Spiritual Meatloaf

Develop Your Personal Spiritual Recipe in Twelve-Step Recovery

Patricia Major

EM Riley Publications

Spiritual Meatloaf
Develop Your Personal Recipe for Spirituality in Twelve-Step Recovery
© 2005 by Patricia Major

All Rights Reserved. No portion of this publication may be reproduced in any manner without the written permission of the publisher.

EM Riley Publications
PO Box 193
Carmel Valley, CA

www.emriley.com

Publisher's Cataloging-in-Publication
(Provided by Quality Books, Inc.)

    Major, Patricia.
     Spiritual meatloaf : develop your personal spiritual recipe in twelve-step recovery / Patricia Major.
     p. cm.
     Includes bibliographical references and index.
     LCCN 2005925591
     ISBN 0-9767023-0-4

     1. Twelve-step programs--Religious aspects.
    2. Spiritual formation.   I. Title.

    BJ1596.M35 2005   201'.76229
                                QBI05-600038

Disclaimers

The stories in this book are derived from members of various Twelve-Step recovery programs. The names have been changed to ensure the privacy of the people involved, and to preserve the tradition of anonymity.

The Twelve Steps are reprinted and adapted and brief excerpts from, *Language of Heart, Alcoholics Anonymous,* "A Newcomer Asks" and "Do You Think You're Different" are reprinted with permission of Alcoholics Anonymous World Services, Inc. (A.A.W.S.) and The A.A. Grapevine, Inc. Permission to reprint and adapt the Twelve Steps and brief excerpts from A.A. material does not mean that A.A.W.S. has reviewed or approved the contents of this publication, or that A.A.W.S. necessarily agrees with the views expressed herein. A.A. is a program of recovery from alcoholism only - use of the Twelve Steps in connection with programs and activities which are patterned after A.A., but which address other problems, or in any other non-A.A. context, does not imply otherwise.

Printed in the Unites States of America
10 9 8 7 6 5 4 3 2 1

TABLE OF CONTENTS

Table of Contents iii

Foreword vii

Introduction xi

So You Think You Hate Meatloaf 15
    What's God Got to Do with It? 18
    The Reason for God in the Steps 24
    Spirituality vs. Religion – The Difference That Makes All the Difference 27
    The Bottom Line – The Least You Can Believe 31
    The Possibilities – Ideas about Higher Power from Others in Recovery 32
    The Turning Point – Where to Go from Here 35

Selecting the Ingredients 37
    Roadblocks – Uncovering Obstacles, Confusion, and Misunderstanding 39
    Salt or Sugar – Identifying Your Basic Beliefs 43
        Exercise 2-1: Questions About Your Beliefs 44
        Exercise 2-2: Watching for Clues 46
    Yesterday and Today – Identifying 47
    Stale Ideas and Old Favorites 47
        Exercise 2-3: Mining for What's True 47
    That Which You Seek – Identifying What's Spiritual 49
        Exercise 2-4: A Few More Questions 50
    Shortcuts – Jumping to Vague Conclusions 51
    Healthy Uncertainty 52
    Acceptance Without Gullibility 52

Creating Your Recipe 55
    Perusing Existing Recipes for Ideas 56
    Multiple Choice Taste-Testing 58
    Mix and Match – Creating Your Own Spiritual Blend 60
        Exercise 3-1: Gathering the Ingredients 60
        Exercise 3-2: Zeroing in on Your Overall Package 66
        Exercise 3-3: Naming Your Spiritual Recipe 66
    Fine Dining – Applying Your Recipe to the Steps 67
        Exercise 3-4: Naming the Focal Point of Your Spiritual Recipe 68
        Exercise 3-5: Reading the Steps with New Eyes 69

Going Meatless – When God Doesn't Fit 71

Disbelief – Using the Steps as an Atheist Without Losing Integrity 72
    Exercise 4-1: Searching for the Words 76
Confusion and Uncertainty – The Advantage of Agnosticism
    in Using the Steps 77
    Exercise 4-2: Using the Big Book 79
Armed and Wary – Approaching Spirituality from Anger and Distrust 80
    Exercise 4-3: Accepting Anger 82
Unique Beliefs – Working with a Sponsor Who
    Has a Different Spiritual Recipe 87
    Exercise 4-4: Sharing About Spirituality 88

Being Vegetarian at the Potluck 91

How Meetings Work – Who's Running the Kitchen 93
Group Conscience – The True Democracy 95
Fear of Brainwashing – Keeping Your Individuality in Recovery 96
    Exercise 5-1: Participating in a Group 99
Listening to Others – Take What You Like and Leave the Rest 100
    Exercise 5-2: Anthropological Expedition 101
Staying Open – Keeping an Open Mind Without
    Losing the One You Have 102
    Exercise 5-3: A Closer Look at Open-Mindedness 103

Meatless, Yet Hearty, Steps 105

Step One: We admitted we were powerless over alcohol – that
    our lives had become unmanageable. 106
Step Two: Came to believe that a Power greater than ourselves
    could restore us to sanity. 108
Step Three: Made a decision to turn our will and our lives over
    to the care of God *as we understood Him*. 110
Step Four: Made a searching and fearless moral inventory of ourselves 112
Step Five: Admitted to God, to ourselves, and to another human
    being the exact nature of our wrongs. 115
Step Six: Were entirely ready to have God remove all these
    defects of character. 116
Step Seven: Humbly asked Him to remove our shortcomings 117
Step Eight: Made a list of all persons we had harmed, and
    became willing to make amends to them all. 118
Step Nine: Made direct amends to such people wherever possible,
    except when to do so would injure them or others. 119
Step Ten: Continued to take personal inventory, and when
    we wrong, promptly admitted it. 121

> Step Eleven: Sought through prayer and meditation to improve our conscious contact with God as we understood Him, praying only for the knowledge of His will for us and the power to carry that out. 123
>
> Step Twelve: Having had a spiritual awakening as the result of these steps, we tried to carry this message to alcoholics and to practice these principles in all our affairs. 125

Cold Leftovers and Suggestions for Reheating 129

The First Spiritual Crisis in Recovery – How to Survive................130
   Exercise 7-1: Act As If..132
I Should Be Better – Fading Spirituality in Long-Term Recovery 133
   Exercise 7-2: Refreshing Your Spiritual Practice..........................136
Dark Night of the Soul – Spiritual Pain..136
   Exercise 7-3: Active Surrendering 139
Refreshers – Keeping Spirituality Interesting.....................................141
A Final Word – Going Out From Here 143

Resources 145

Programs for Recovery..145
   Twelve-Step Recovery Programs..145
   Alternative Recovery Programs 146
Books 147
   Twelve-Step Program Literature..147
   Other Twelve Step Books 148
   Alternative Recovery Books 148
   Spiritual Growth and Exploration 149
   World Religions..150
Websites of Interest...150
   World Religions and Spirituality 150
   Alternative Recovery 150

Index...151

About the Author... 155

Order Form.. 156

Foreword

I am glad to see that a book like this exists, and wish it had been available when I was first getting into Twelve-Step recovery. It might have made it less frightening for me to continue to attend meetings, knowing that I was not the only one who sees spirituality without God. And I think it might help some others stick around who would otherwise leave, without understanding that they really can believe whatever feels right for them.

I am not a famous person at all. I am simply a person who entered recovery as an atheist and wondered how I would survive the spiritual aspects of the Twelve-Step program. I had run out of other options, including nonsectarian recovery programs, and I was desperate to stop using and drinking. I flipped a coin to make a decision; heads for suicide and tails for the AA meeting down the street. Tails it was.

It may be that it was just the right timing or that I had finally, really, given up. I will never know for sure, but one thing I do know: I have been successful in my recovery by using AA and the Twelve Steps, and am happy to say I have been clean and sober for several years.

When I was asked to write this foreword, I wondered how my words could possibly make a difference. I am not a licensed therapist, a world-renowned clergy person, or even a more prominent member of AA or another Twelve-Step program. I was quickly reminded about the equality of all Twelve-Step members. Nobody is higher or lower in the echelon than anyone else. And the Twelve-Step programs do not have a "national spokesperson" or official representatives. Every single member is just as qualified as the next, and every single member is entitled to his or her opinion about how the Twelve Steps work for them.

That equality is what I credit for allowing me to use the Twelve Steps for my recovery. It keeps us from becoming all-knowing experts, which might then result in rules and dogma. Fortunately, there were, and are, no rules. I was not forced to believe in anyone else's idea of spirituality. I was welcomed into the group even before I was sure I wanted to be welcomed. And I am still welcomed today, despite my opposition to the idea of an external personality called God.

I am not pretending it was easy for me to swallow the God talk and the Judeo-Christian concepts that permeated the meetings and literature. If I hadn't been desperate, I would have run out before the end of the first meeting that I attended. I sat silently with my arms crossed and judged every word I heard. Nobody was going to force God or religion down my throat, although I was afraid if they did, I might give in and pretend to go along just to be a part of the group.

That did not happen. As I became comfortable enough to talk to other people, they assured me that I could use any concept of spirituality I chose. Even spirituality itself was optional, although without it, I was told, I would be choked off from the essence of the Program. It was all up to me. My skepticism gradually turned into trust, and the defensiveness gave way to a sense of freedom that I had never before felt. It was really okay to be myself and to believe what I really believed.

I still wince on occasion when I hear someone talk about God the Father, but I have learned that, just as others let me have my opinions, I can let others have theirs. Nobody can prove they're right, so whatever works for each person is what matters.

Meanwhile, I have developed my own brand of spirituality. I follow my values, I believe in the invisible power of love, and I have heard others talk about God being Love, so maybe we're not so different, except for the words we use.

There is nothing else on earth like the Twelve Steps, and I often wish the entire planet could use them. We'd probably get along much better. But for now, they are available to those of us who are desperate enough to reach out for help in recovery. If you are one of those people, congratulations for having the courage to get help. I believe the ideas in this book can help you find the spirituality that is uniquely yours.

— *An Anonymous Member of Alcoholics Anonymous*

Is A.A. a religious society?

A.A. is not a religious society, since it requires no definite religious belief as a condition of membership. Although it has been endorsed and approved by many religious leaders, it is not allied with any organization or sect. Included in its membership are Catholics, Protestants, Jews, members of other major religious bodies, agnostics, and atheists.

The A.A. program of recovery from alcoholism is undeniably based on acceptance of certain spiritual values. The individual member is free to interpret those values as he or she thinks best, or not to think about them at all.

Most members, before turning to A.A., had already admitted that they could not control their drinking. Alcohol had become a power greater than themselves, and it had been accepted on those terms. A.A. suggests that to achieve and maintain sobriety, alcoholics need to accept and depend upon another Power recognized as greater than themselves. Some alcoholics choose to consider the A.A. group itself as the power greater than themselves; for many others, this Power is God – *as they, individually, understand Him;* still others rely upon entirely different concepts of a Higher Power.

Some alcoholics, when they first turn to A.A., have definite reservations about accepting any concept of a Power greater than themselves. Experience shows that, if they will keep an open mind on the subject and keep coming to A.A. meetings, they are not likely to have too difficult a time in working out an acceptable solution to this distinctly personal problem.

– *44 Questions*: Copyright © 1952 by Works Publishing, Inc. (Now A.A. World Services, Inc.), taken from the Alcoholics Anonymous website: www.alcoholics-anonymous.org

Introduction

This book is for anyone who is in spiritual conflict or confusion about Twelve-Step recovery. It will have something to offer you if any of the following statements are true:

1. You are new to recovery and:
   - Have doubts about the logic of spirituality.
   - Fear brainwashing.
   - Wonder what you're *supposed* to believe in recovery.
   - Oppose the idea of God or religion.
   - Suspect the idea of God is a psychological crutch.
   - Feel angry with God or the clergy.
   - Worry about whether your beliefs will fit or be accepted.
   - Looking for a way to make sense of your beliefs.
   - Are an atheist or agnostic.
   - Cannot find a sponsor who believes what you believe.

2. You have been in recovery for a while and:
   - Feel disconnected from your Higher Power.
   - Think your ideas about God no longer fit.
   - Wish to find a church to reinforce your faith.
   - Want to find or strengthen your inner connection.
   - Desire a deeper experience of the Steps.

If any of those descriptions applies to you, you will find some peace of mind in these pages.

Although some people (both inside and outside of the Twelve-Step programs) might try to tell you otherwise, *you do not need to believe in God* to succeed in your recovery.

While tinkering with faith seems like risky business, recovery demands taking a closer look. The desperation that caused you to seek out recovery may also compel you to revise your spiritual beliefs or attitudes. By applying honesty, open-mindedness, and willingness to this search, you can reinvent not only your spirituality, but your entire outlook on life.

ϒϒϒ

> *"We find that no one need have difficulty with the spirituality of the program. Willingness, honesty and open-mindedness are the essentials of recovery. But these are indispensable."*
> – from *Alcoholics Anonymous* p 567, Fourth Edition.

Even if you already have firm ideas about God and religion, entering Twelve Step recovery may provide a monumental spiritual challenge. *Spiritual Meatloaf* is a tool for guiding you through such a challenge with your integrity intact.

Whether your quest is brand new or ongoing, this book guides without force. It provides a road map for you to uncover your own personal path without insisting that you change what you think or believe. By clarifying the way Twelve Step programs use the concept of a Higher Power, this book eliminates conflicts with your personal beliefs, regardless of the way you define your spirituality. The tools and suggestions in this book take a logical approach, and if followed, provide you with a sense of confidence in who you are and where you stand in regard to God in recovery.

Chapter One examines the way the Twelve Steps include God, what the Steps really expect you to believe, and the amazing loophole that takes the pressure off.

Chapters Two and Three guide you as you evaluate your own beliefs and discard worn out ideas.

Chapter Four addresses ways of overcoming specific challenges to spirituality, including atheism, agnosticism, anger, and beliefs that differ from the traditional.

Chapter Five provides a brief overview of the inner workings of Twelve-Step groups and discusses the issue of retaining individuality while participating in a group.

Chapter Six carries you through each of the Twelve Steps as you apply your own personal spiritual recipe.

Chapter Seven will be especially helpful if you are already established in recovery, but find your spiritual or religious foundation crumbling or worn out. This chapter helps you revise your faith by identifying what still works, eliminating broken ideas, and finding new ones.

May this book be a spiritual compass as you trudge the road of happy destiny.

Basic Meatloaf Recipe

2 tsp vegetable oil (or olive oil or no oil or cod liver oil)
1 med onion, chopped (optional)
2 garlic cloves minced chopped, or whole (or use none or lots more)
2 large eggs (or not; or 4 quail eggs, or 6 egg whites)
1/2 tsp dried thyme (or 1 hour fresh time, or postpone indefinitely)
1 tsp salt (sea salt, salt from tears, or salt substitute)
1/2 tsp ground black pepper (or mixed corns, or none or more)
2 tsp Dijon mustard (or hot Chinese or bright yellow or none)
2 tsp Worcestershire sauce (or chili sauce or salsa or ketchup)
1/4 teaspoon hot sauce (or cold sauce or room temp sauce)
1/2 cup milk (or soy milk or water or heavy cream)
1 lb ground chuck (or tofu or ground turkey or chicken livers)
1/2 lb ground pork (optional)
1/2 lb ground veal (optional)
¼ cup raisins (optional)
1 cup frogs' legs (optional)
2/3 cup crushed saltine crackers, about 16 (or 1 loaf day-old bread)
1/3 cup minced parsley (or cilantro or something else or nothing)

Use a utensil or your hands or feet to mix some or all ingredients until they reach the desired consistency. If you wish, you may put the mixture in a pan or directly on the oven shelf, or simply eat it out of the bowl. Bake it, eat it raw, or fry it in a skillet. Top with or without ketchup, bacon strips, semi-sweet chocolate pieces, or mashed potatoes.

Bon appetite!

CHAPTER ONE

SO YOU THINK YOU HATE MEATLOAF

*"Did you ever have the feeling that you wanted to go,
and still have the feeling that you wanted to stay?"*
– sung by Jimmy Durante in
"The Man Who Came to Dinner" (1942).

This isn't really about meatloaf, of course. It's about dealing with spirituality in Twelve-Step recovery, and whether or not you want to include God or religion in your spiritual mix.

The word "God" shows up a lot in the Twelve Steps. This causes many people facing recovery to feel nervous, disgusted, or even hopeless. For any number of reasons, as much as you want to jump into the healing waters of recovery, you might feel you've just discovered those waters are ice cold, too cold to survive.

If you are saying to yourself, "I'd rather die than to turn myself into a cult member," just keep reading. Far from being at a dead end, you may find that Twelve-Step recovery is the only place you can be absolutely true to yourself and to your own beliefs.

You do not need to believe in anything that doesn't fit for you. You don't need to mold your brain to anyone else's idea of a Higher Power, creed, code, or spirituality. The only requirement for membership in any of Twelve-Step recovery programs is a *desire to stop* the self-destructive behavior that got you there. That phrase, in one form or another, is part of every Twelve-Step program. It includes absolutely no requirement that you believe in God. In fact, the Steps were deliberately designed to include a large "spiritual loophole" that allows anyone, of any persuasion, to participate successfully in Twelve-Step recovery.

ᛉᛉᛉ

> *"The majority of A.A. members believe that we have found the solution to our drinking problem not through individual willpower, but through a power greater than ourselves. However, everyone defines this power as he or she wishes. Many people call it God, others think it is the A.A. group, still others don't believe in it at all. There is room in A.A. for people of all shades of belief and nonbelief."*
> – from the AA pamphlet: *A Newcomer Asks*

This book is about that spiritual loophole and how you can use it in recovery. While the idea of spirituality is a core element of the Twelve Steps, the truth is that you can define exactly what this means to you – on your own terms. It means there is room for just about anyone – even if you are an agnostic or an atheist, even if you are repelled by traditional religions or the various names attributed to God, or if you once had faith that you let go of for any reason. By taking the Twelve Step Programs at their word – that you can develop your own personal spirituality – you can successfully override, and therefore come to terms with, "the God thing."

What exactly do the Twelve-Step programs mean by "spirituality"? Most dictionaries link the word to religious ideas, but there is nothing that says you cannot define it in your own way, as long as it is meaningful to *you*. For example, one friend in recovery describes his spirituality as "my own personal set of values and my commitment to live by them." Another defines it as her "relationship with the world."

You get to decide all of this on your own terms, and nobody can tell you otherwise. That's another part of the loophole – *there are no rules*. In fact, you can put this book down right now, ignore the idea of spirituality altogether, and still be part of any Twelve-Step recovery program. However, if you prefer doing things the easiest way possible, keep reading. The Twelve Steps have worked for millions of people, and you can be one of them.

One recovering alcoholic describes the individual journey this way: "While I was drinking, I did a lot of evil things. I don't do those anymore. I do other little things, but they're not major like they used to be. As long as I am on this path, I can be a better person – to my wife, to my children, to my friends – and I just feel better. So, for me, this is a spiritual journey, and I believe it's the answer. It's not money and power and all that stuff that makes me happy. I needed to be here with these little simple things, and over time, beautiful things have happened. Everyone is on a separate journey, and they have to hit the wall – to find out that what they're doing isn't working. It's different for everybody."

What's God Got to Do with It?

As you have seen, the word "God" is everywhere in the Twelve Steps. Even where the particular word is not used, it is frequently implied, as shown in the original version of the Steps, the Twelve Steps of Alcoholics Anonymous (references to God are in bold):

1. We admitted we were powerless over alcohol – that our lives had become unmanageable.
2. Came to believe that a **Power greater than ourselves** could restore us to sanity.
3. Made a decision to turn our will and our lives over to the care of **God** as we understood **Him**.
4. Made a searching and fearless moral inventory of ourselves.
5. Admitted to **God**, to ourselves, and to another human being the exact nature of our wrongs.

6. Were entirely ready to have **God** remove all these defects of character.
7. Humbly asked **Him** to remove our shortcomings.
8. Made a list of all persons we had harmed, and became willing to make amends to them all.
9. Made direct amends to such people wherever possible, except when to do so would injure them or others.
10. Continued to take personal inventory and when we were wrong promptly admitted it.
11. Sought through prayer and meditation to improve our conscious contact with **God**, as we understood **Him**, praying only for knowledge of **His** will for us and the power to carry that out.
12. Having had a spiritual awakening as the result of these Steps, we tried to carry this message to alcoholics, and to practice these principles in all our affairs.

Copyright © A.A. World Services, Inc.

What do these steps expect or even require you to do with "God" or a "Power greater than ourselves"? Thanks to the wisdom of the earliest members of AA, it's up to you to decide.

Maybe you are like many others in Twelve-Step recovery who are looking at the Twelve Steps with initial wariness or confusion about the God concept. Or, you've been in recovery for a while and thought you had it sorted out, but are not as sure as you once were.

You may also be in another frame of mind: You may feel you have lost every shred of meaning in your life, especially any ideas of faith or spirituality. You may be feeling so much pain that you can't bear to go on, except that you somehow do. You may be one of those people who has ended up in recovery without really knowing why (except for the disasters you've experienced). The idea of God may seem irrelevant, ridiculous, or even abominable. If this is where you find yourself, *you've probably ended up in the one place where you can find something true and believable to hold onto.* In any of the Twelve-Step programs, you can believe whatever you choose, no matter how strange or personal.

That feeling of pointlessness and the inability to believe in God is exactly where **Regina** began her recovery:

"I walked into a meeting in so much pain that I didn't even notice the large poster of the Twelve Steps and their references to God hanging on the wall at the front of the room! If I had suspected God would be put in my face, I probably would have left, even though I didn't have much energy left for resistance to anything."

"God had lost all meaning for me. Growing up, I had been force-fed ideas of a moody and condemning God. And the older I got, the less religion made sense to me. By the time I reached my teens, I was skipping out on Sunday Mass, hiding out with the other 'misfits and trouble-makers' in the schoolyard behind the Church."

"Life in the 50's was supposed to be 'swell' – all Disney and Leave It to Beaver. But mine didn't seem so good. No matter how hard I tried, I wasn't happy. And, after many unsuccessful attempts to get things 'under control,' I had run myself into the ground. By the time I sought recovery, I had dismantled a second marriage and left my adolescent son behind as I rode off into the sunset on the back of a motorcycle driven by someone else's drunken husband. I had hurt lots of people, including myself, and the shame and guilt were destroying what was left of me. On one of my worst days, I stumbled onto a book that pointed out the insanity of living the way I was and led me to investigate Twelve-Step recovery."

"Thank God nobody at my first recovery meeting tried to tell me what I needed to believe. That first group did contain some church-going members, but the group as a whole stayed close to the Twelve Traditions and upheld the idea of 'attraction rather than promotion.' I think it was because of the open-minded attitude of the people there that I was able to stay around and eventually uncover my own spirituality rather than having to choose between pretending or leaving."

"My skepticism toward all things religious, even with people telling me I was free to define my own path, made it difficult to get through those Steps the first time through. I was trying to redefine the concept of God in a way that fit for me, but emotional residue of the 'old God' was still built up inside of me. My religious training had started at such a young age that the ideas seemed to be embedded in my cells. I felt bogged down, dishonest about my participation in recovery, and resistant to doing the Steps."

"For several years, I explored various churches and philosophies while I continued to attend Program meetings. I traveled to Ireland to attend a writing workshop, and while there, explored the Catholicism I had abandoned years before. The ritual – the incense, the music, the Latin chants – restored some appreciation of the mystery I had embraced as a child, but the politics and dogma still left me cold."

"I later traveled with a school group to Nepal to study Buddhism and to submerge myself in a culture that openly practiced spirituality. Again, the rituals pulled me in, but some of the precepts didn't fit with my beliefs and values. I was attending Twelve-Step meetings during some of my travels, and while I felt welcomed wherever I went, I also felt like I was living a lie because of my nebulous, undefined spirituality."

"It was then that I received one of the best pieces of advice I ever got: *Stop thinking so much about it*, and be willing to admit that you can't figure it out with logic. That advice motivated me to give up on all of my old arguments about whether God exists or whether the whole idea was simply man-made wishful thinking. I didn't have the answers, and nobody else did either."

"Over time, I came to terms with my own version of spirituality, and it turned out to be something entirely outside the limits of those old arguments. I don't know whether it could ever fit for anyone else, and it doesn't really matter, anyway."

I know many other people who have designed their own spirituality. **Michael** likes to say he belongs to the church of "Michaelanity." He explains that while he got the idea of the name from Christianity, it's his very own personal version of religion. He says there's only one parking space and only one place to sit. It belongs to no one else.

It doesn't matter what approach you take. But if you want to be successful with the Twelve Steps, the easiest way would be to find what works for you and let that be your foundation. Anything that's meaningful to you will be fine, whether it's logical, mystical, or completely self-invented and unique.

If you are someone who relies primarily on logic, it may help to read the next section, *The Reason for God in the Steps*, which discusses why, if believing in God is not necessary for recovery, the idea of God is used in the Twelve Steps.

If you're not the logical type, you may actually be better off than most. Some ideas are just not defined by logic, and for many people, that's *exactly* where their spirituality comes in.

ϒϒϒ

"These ideas that we have about how things are or how they should be exist no where else except in our own minds."
— Cheri Huber, Center for the Practice
of Zen Buddhist Meditation,
The Key: and the Name of the Key is Willingness

The Reason for God in the Steps

If believing in God is not required for using the Steps, why do the Steps mention it in so many places? The first consideration is based on the history of Alcoholics Anonymous, the original Twelve-Step program. A lot of the groundwork for AA was laid by the Oxford Group, an evangelical Episcopal movement whose focus was to restore the spirit of early Christianity. The meetings were simple, without much in the way of rituals or pageantry, and its members were striving for the practice of universal spiritual values, including the "Four Absolutes" of honesty, purity, unselfishness, and love. They also practiced meditation, which they called "quiet time," and the sharing of and restitution for the harms they had done. These people were looking to the highest and best parts of themselves, and having been raised in a time and place where "God" was the name of the Highest Power, it was only natural that the name and the concept was used. Many of AA's spiritual concepts were taken from the Oxford Group, and thus it was that the Steps included a similar concept of God.

Even in those early days of AA, some very vocal agnostics were part of the group to which Bill Wilson brought his first draft of the Twelve Steps. As Bill says in *The Language of the Heart* (AA Grapevine, Inc., New York, 1988), "Our agnostic contingent, speared by Hank P. and Jim B., finally convinced us that we must make it easier for people like themselves by using such terms as 'a

Higher Power' or 'God as we understand him.' Those expressions, as we so well know today, have proved lifesavers for many an alcoholic."

There is also a story, which has been both refuted and confirmed by various "reliable" sources, that when the printer sent a pre-press copy of the first version of *Alcoholics Anonymous* to Bill Wilson, Bill's secretary noticed that the phrase "as we understood" had been inadvertently left out of the printer's proof. Reportedly, Bill told her to let it go, that it was too much trouble to re-do the proofs at that late stage. She reminded him of the long discussions that had produced the phrase, and he finally agreed that it ought to be included after all.

No matter how that phrase found its way into the Twelve Steps, the word "God" was meant to be interpreted as the individual saw fit. There is no need to take the word "God" literally, and in fact, it's preferable that you do not. Let it be a placeholder for whatever your idea of spirituality may be. *Seeing that word through new eyes is the most honest approach you can take, and could even mean the difference between success and failure in recovery.*

One other very important reason for being true to your own beliefs is revealed in hindsight by those who have experienced success in recovery. Part of their success was a sense of relief – the pain of living was replaced by a sense of meaning and a new sense of power. The first of the Twelve Steps asks only that you admit that you couldn't figure things out and make them work. The remaining Steps, by using the idea of God, are simply recommending that you be open to a different way of seeing the world and how you fit into it.

ϒϒϒ

> *"My friend suggested what then seemed a novel idea. He said, 'Why don't you choose your own conception of God?' That statement hit me hard. It melted the icy intellectual mountain in whose shadow I had lived and shivered many years. I stood in the sunlight at last. It was only a matter of being willing to believe in a Power greater than myself. Nothing more was required of me to make my beginning."* — Bill W. in *Alcoholics Anonymous*

If you are seeking recovery, you are seeking a new way of interacting with the universe. Logic dictates that you cannot continue on the same course with the same attitudes. Unless you establish a new or more focused set of ideas about your existence and what it means, you'll be stuck on your old path. This is the point of having God in the Steps: In this culture, the concept of God is the one most commonly used when we talk of a meaningful, inner perspective. Even for those who don't literally believe in God, we can use those words as a kind of shorthand for the inner awareness that we are not in control of the world. Unless you are certain that you understand every aspect of our existence and can clearly explain the meaning of life, you can probably accept that there is some mystery to it all. You could even use this idea to explain your spirituality. As Iris Dement sings, she doesn't have the answers, so she'll just "let the Mystery be." And many people call this God.

Spirituality vs. Religion – The Difference That Makes All the Difference

What's the difference between spirituality and religion? Take a look at parts of the definitions of *spirit*, *spiritual*, and *religion* from *Webster's Ninth New Collegiate Dictionary*:

spirit from the Latin spiritus, lit., breath; to blow, breathe; an animating or vital principle held to give life to physical organisms; a supernatural being or essence; the immaterial intelligent or sentient part of a person; the activating or essential principle influencing a person; a special attitude or frame of mind; a distillate (often used in place of alcohol); an alcoholic solution of a volatile substance; God.

spiritual of or relating to the spirit; of or relating to sacred matters; concerned with religious values; of or relating to supernatural beings or phenomena.

religion from the Latin religio, reverence; the service and worship of God of the supernatural; archaic: scrupulous conformity; a cause, principle, or system of beliefs held to with ardor and faith.

At first glance, you can see a few similarities. In each of the above definitions, God and the supernatural are mentioned. However, in this particular dictionary, many of the words in the definitions are different from one to the next. This is not by accident. While there's usually some spirituality in religion, the idea of religion is very different from spirituality. Religion is a group system; spirituality is a frame of mind.

ϓϓϓ

> *"Religion is concerned with God's relationship with the universe; spirituality is focused on the way a person sees his own place in the universe."* – from *Steps of Transformation* by Father Meletios Webber, an Orthodox Priest

The way we see the world, as shaped by our genes and our experiences, is the basic foundation for our spirituality. The idea of the sacred – something accorded great value and respect – is left to each person to define. No matter what you believe is valuable and worthy of respect, you can combine these ingredients to create a "spiritual recipe."

Even if you have no belief in anything supernatural or beyond the scientifically proven, you can see that life exists. The first definition of the word spirit in this particular dictionary describes it as "an animating or vital principle held to give life to physical organisms." This means that, whether you believe that life emanates from a supernatural source or whether you think it started as a chemical reaction, you can still acknowledge that something caused it. The word "Cause" is often substituted for the word "God" by people who shun traditional religious references to a deity.

If you simply do not want to think about any of these spiritual or religious matters, ask yourself whether you are willing to take an honest look at what you really believe. It's one thing to be adamantly individualistic (in this book, it is considered a wonderful quality!). But, if you would rather die or have your old life back than to define your own idea of spirituality, consider whether you are being controlled by your need to be *against* someone or something else. It's a strange way to be controlled, but it can still keep you from making your own, unbiased decisions.

Complete resistance to identifying what you believe might also mean that you are simply not ready to stop the behavior that brought you to recovery. You might, consciously or unconsciously, be looking for an excuse to keep fooling yourself.

Finally, rejection of this kind of introspection may mean that you have a clearly defined set of beliefs about life that cannot fit the ideas presented in this book.

Whatever your reasons, if you cannot come to terms with *any* type of spirituality, even by your own definition, you still don't need to give up on the idea of recovery. You may be perfectly able to use the Twelve Steps while you avoid or ignore the spiritual aspects. And you may find another recovery program that better fits for you (see the *Resources* section at the back of this book).

There is a clear and simple motto used in the Program: *Take what you like and leave the rest for future reference.* You can take this at face value. No one with any amount of successful recovery will tell you that you can't stick around just because you're not "spiritual."

Spirituality does not *require* God. Our ability to communicate with all parts of the Globe has given us information about other cultures, confirming that:

- The Judeo-Christian God is not the God to which most people pray.
- Many religions worship other "aspects" of God, such as nature.
- Some religions have no concept of God at all.

People's ideas about spirituality, religion, and God often depend on where they were born, to which parents, and in which century. It also means that, unless a few Judeo-Christians are the only ones in need of recovery, the Twelve Steps need to be flexible about spirituality if they are going to work for people all over the world. Fortunately, this is the case. As of January 2003, Alcoholics Anonymous meetings, as well as many other Twelve-Step meetings, occur in more than 150 countries (from Alcoholics Anonymous World Services website) and this number continues to grow.

ϓϓϓ

> *"While A.A. has restored thousands of poor Christians to their churches, and has made believers out of atheists and agnostics, it has also made good A.A.'s out of those belonging to the Buddhist, Islamic, and Jewish faiths. For example, we question very much whether our Buddhist members in Japan would ever have joined this Society had A.A. officially stamped itself a strictly Christian movement.*

> *You can easily convince yourself of this by imagining that A.A. started among the Buddhists and that they then told you you couldn't join them unless you became a Buddhist, too. If you were a Christian alcoholic under these circumstances, you might well turn your face to the wall and die."*
> — Bill Wilson, Letter 1954

If the Twelve Step Programs did not stand behind the words, "As we understood him," they could never have grown and helped so many millions all over the world. This is an indisputable fact: No one group or religion "owns" these Steps, and if they did, the Twelve Step groups would whither away and die to all but a few.

The Bottom Line – The Least You Can Believe

No matter how you look at it, the idea of God, or at least spirituality, is in the Twelve Steps. Does this mean you can't use the Steps if you can't find or participate in spirituality? And what, if anything, is required?

Technically, *nothing is required.* Nobody has the authority or the right to tell you what you must think or believe. There's another way: Be willing to let go of your resistance. This doesn't mean turning into a mindless sponge with no opinions or thoughts of your own. It's about attitude more than anything else. Keeping an open mind does not mean placing yourself in danger of being swept up in religious fervor. But, if you are *willing* to take a look at new ideas, you may succeed in recovery – and you can do it with your own personal set of beliefs intact.

Most Twelve-Step meetings announce that "the only requirement for membership is a *desire to stop...*" drinking, using, or whatever self-destructive behavior that particular meeting focuses on. That's it. That word "desire" represents the bottom line. You already know that the desire to quit was worthless by itself. This means that recovery had better be offering something more than just a group of people who *desire*. The real problem seems to be finding a way to change desire into reality.

This is exactly where the idea of a "Higher Power" comes in. Since your willpower obviously wasn't enough, you need another form or source of power. This alternate source, no matter how you define it, needs to exist or there is no hope. Whatever you believe, some idea exists in your mind about who you are and how you relate to the world – whether it's swirling electrons, total chaos, natural law, or God. If you haven't been able to quit on your own, you can turn to this source of power. This is your spirituality.

The Possibilities – Ideas about Higher Power from Others in Recovery

Jack claims to be adrift without a spiritual anchor, yet we have had hours-long conversations about spirituality. He no longer feels resentment toward the God he knew in training for the Catholic priesthood, he just doesn't have the same ideas about who or what God is. He's still searching for the words to use when he refers to a Higher Power, and isn't even sure the word God will ever fit. He just knows there's a mystery that he cannot fully explain. The rest of his strength seems to come from the groups and the people he has met in the Program.

Derek points out that nothing in the Twelve Steps says you need to believe in God. The Steps tell you which actions to take, but not what to believe. Without knowing what he means by "God," he takes the actions as if he knew. For example, when he turns his will and his life over to the care of a Higher Power, Derek tells himself that since he is obviously not able to control everything in the universe, it's easy to imagine that a power greater than himself exists. He just uses that idea whenever Higher Power or God is mentioned.

Li says that, "When one considers that generally Buddhism is a non-theist spiritual path based upon the development of human potential motivated by a desire to benefit others," she is not surprised that the Twelve Steps work well for her. When Judeo-Christian prayers make her uncomfortable, which they still do, she repeats the Medicine Buddha mantra under her breath.

Joan, a woman who grew up a Pagan, was ready to run when she saw the spiritual basis of the Program. "What kept me in my seat was the desperate fear that if I picked up one more time, I would die." She eventually came to see that "… the spiritual principals of recovery are far-reaching and non-denominational."

Paul, an atheist, states that "One of the greatest things I ever heard in AA is that we all have faith if we have fear, because fear is faith that everything will go horribly wrong. Thus, if I can have faith in the negative, why can't I have faith in the positive? This is the kind of faith that has proof that it works without beads, drinking red wine on Sundays, or getting on your knees."

And **Joe**, a Native American, talks of discarding the creator of his own ideas (ego) and traveling on a path given to him by his ancestors "… made visible to me by the Twelve Steps." He participates in ritual and ceremony, including Twelve-Step meetings, "not to impress God, but to humble myself before the Creator of the way things are."

You are completely free to see, or not to see, your own Higher Power. Free to use whatever word or phrase reminds you of what you believe. You do not need to know what gravity is in order to believe that you are securely fastened to the Earth's surface. You do not need to understand the workings of electricity in order to flip the light switch. Probably most who are entering recovery are on shaky spiritual ground. Those who are fortunate are able to stay around and listen and learn until they grasp their own, personal ideas of what the words God and Higher Power mean to them. There is nothing to fight against, and there are no rules to break. Whatever you believe, you can probably find a way to weave it safely and with integrity into the Twelve Steps.

ϒϒϒ

> *"As soon as we admitted the possible existence of a Creative Intelligence, a Spirit of the Universe underlying the totality of things, we began to be possessed of a new sense of power and direction, provided we took other simple steps...To us, the Realm of the Spirit is broad, roomy, all inclusive; never exclusive or forbidding to those who earnestly seek. It is open, we believe, to all men."* – from *Alcoholics Anonymous*

The Turning Point – Where to Go from Here

Now you need to decide between using the rest of this book to sort out your own spirituality or moving on to some other way of recovery. If you think you can keep an open mind, or at least be tolerant of the ideas of God and spirituality in the Twelve Steps, the exercises and ideas in the next chapter can help you zero in on what you really believe.

You will have a very good chance of recovery if, in addition to looking at your own spirituality, you also follow these suggestions:

- Talk to others, including your sponsor.
- Read some of the other books out there.
- Go to a variety of meetings and listen carefully for similarities.
- Follow the leads that turn up as you continue to search for your own spirituality.

If you are just not able to get any sense of meaning from this or other parts of this book, you can still use the Twelve Step programs for recovery, simply by observing the process in others.

Finally, if you absolutely cannot consider the possibility of anything beyond the realm of your own logic and self-sufficiency, you may need to look for other recovery possibilities. The Twelve Steps are a good way to achieve recovery, but they are not the only way. See *Resources* toward the end of this book for some other ideas.

CHAPTER TWO

SELECTING THE INGREDIENTS

*"To be doomed to an alcoholic death or to live on a spiritual
basis are not always easy alternatives to face."*
— ©1976AAWS, *Alcoholics Anonymous*, p 44

You are not expected to believe anything in particular about God, spirituality, or religion in order to succeed with the Twelve Steps. You are not even expected to know what you do or don't believe or to be consistent about what you believe. Knowing where you stand however, can make it *easier* to use the Steps.

This is not some underhanded way of tricking you into being "saved," nor is it some kind of slick brainwashing technique. It simply means that if you consciously become aware of how you feel and what you think about life, you'll be able to sort out your values and beliefs, and as a result, you will have some guiding principles to live by. It's good to have some *reason* to choose a way of living that contributes to recovery.

Clarifying your beliefs is *not about trying to define God*. In fact, many people believe it is impossible to use the human mind to define a Higher Power. If that power were small enough to be grasped by our logic, it would not be all that great.

ϓϓϓ

> "*If you could prove to me logically that there is a personal God and I don't think you can – I still would not be inclined to talk to a presence I couldn't feel. If I could prove to you logically that there is no God – and I know I can't – your true faith would not be shaken. In other words, matters of faith lie entirely outside the realm of reason. Is there anything beyond the realm of human reason? Yes, I believe there is. Something .*" – from the AA pamphlet: *Do You Think You're Different – Jan's Story*

What then does it mean to "clarify" your beliefs? Rather than trying to help you define (or discredit) God, the focus here is on identifying the ideas you already have about spirituality and religion. It doesn't matter whether your ideas are positive, negative, or neutral. Most (but not all) people get into recovery with at least some preconceived ideas or opinions about religion. This chapter will help you sort out what you believe, and then help you to decide what is worth keeping and what is no longer useful for you.

This chapter includes ideas and tools to help you:

- identify what you believe about spirituality, God, and religion.
- explore your existing beliefs in light of how they fit for you at this stage of your life.
- review existing thoughts and philosophies from various parts of the world.
- feel comfortable about and confident in your own spiritual recipe.

Roadblocks – Uncovering Obstacles, Confusion, and Misunderstanding

The spiritual obstacles faced by alcoholics and addicts entering Twelve-Step Programs are not new. The early founders of AA (Alcoholics Anonymous) had many heated discussions about how to apply spiritual principles without forcing people into religion. Throughout the book *Alcoholics Anonymous* (also called the "Big Book"), they frequently discuss the spiritual challenges and devote an entire chapter – "We Agnostics" – to the topic of disbelief in or resistance to spirituality.

However, reading the Big Book (or the equivalent book for your particular program) isn't always much help when you've been abused in the name of religion or have become cynical because of encounters with people in positions of religious authority.

Don's resistance had a solid foundation: "From kindergarten through the first year of high school, my parochial schooling was conducted by teachers who acted out their human failings in the name of religious authority. Children were publicly shamed for not remembering the capital city of a foreign country, or beaten for staring lazily out a springtime window. Other situations were so ridiculous as to be humorous, such as my first grade experience in which one nun told me to throw away my bologna sandwich because it contained meat (it was Friday), and the next nun had me pull it from the trash because wasting was a sin."

"In later years, hypocrites, users, and abusers were abundant in every church I explored. I developed a strong and biting cynicism. At one point, I had a large sign on my front door warning people not to bother knocking if they were trying to sell religion."

"It's no surprise, then, that when I first tried to approach Twelve-Step recovery, the word 'God' stood squarely in my way. I thought I was being witty and righteous when I began to parrot a few others who described themselves as 'recovering Catholics.' "

"I began to read the Big Book because it was recommended by one of my first sponsors. When I got to 'We Agnostics,' I skimmed through it the way I scanned the business page in the local paper – lots of words that meant very little to me. Surrounded by people who talked about God or their Higher Power, I felt misplaced at best and hypocritical at worst. My spiritual aloofness felt like a secret but I stayed busy 'working on recovery.' "

"I did hear someone talk about the concept of 'God, as we understood God.' But for me, even having permission to redefine God wasn't much help. The 'definition' of God had been deeply embedded in my mind, and no matter what I tried to think, those old ideas were stuck inside of me. My mind said one thing – that I could have the idea of spirituality on my own terms – but my gut kept telling me to watch out for that judgmental God I had grown up with."

Alicia talks about how the judgmental God of her childhood kept her from understanding the openness of Twelve-Step spirituality: "Even an early childhood prayer felt ominous to me:

> Now I lay me down to sleep
> I pray the Lord my soul to keep
> If I should die before I wake
> I pray the Lord my soul to take.

Implied in this innocent verse was the idea that somehow God might decide ***not*** to keep me safe. And with the mind of a child, I believed I had to ask for safety and protection, and that I had to be perfect to get it. Since there was no way I knew of to be perfect, I slowly moved away from the rigorous demands of God."

"The chapter 'We Agnostics' in the AA Big Book is brilliantly written, even inspired. Yet my resistance was so strong that I was incapable of getting its message."

"I figured if other people could stop destroying themselves, I could too. I didn't realize that people had already developed their own spiritual inner connections. All I could see was that they were going to meetings, saying the right things, and somehow holding themselves together. I thought they were doing this by self will and their ties to the group."

Daniel's stumbling block was a wariness of being told what to believe: "I believed God was a fabrication of the human mind. People could believe all they wanted, but I brushed it aside because I 'knew better.' I strongly doubted the sincerity of anything or anyone who said I did not have to believe in anyone else's God. This included the words on page 46 of the 4th edition of the Big Book of *Alcoholics Anonymous*: 'When, therefore, we speak to you of God, we mean your own conception of God. This applies, too, to other spiritual expressions which you find in this book. Do not let any prejudice you may have against spiritual terms deter you from honestly asking yourself what they mean to you.' "

"Even so clearly spelled out, the word God made me suspicious. They referred to 'Him' and described God in terms of human characteristics. It not only didn't fit for me, it caused me to run further in the other direction."

"It took years for me to realize the truth: *No one, inside or outside of recovery, can tell me what to think or what to believe.* There is no authority waiting to trick me into having a religious experience. I really am free to create my own personal spirituality and to translate the word God in my own way. And when people in recovery talk about God as if it were the same for us all, I now know that they mean well but are mistaken."

ϒϒϒ

> *"... if this spiritual treatment becomes too religious, it hardly gets a chance to start. To be successful, the treatment has to be based on a spirituality that stops short of blossoming into a religious faith. It has to be a spirituality in which God Himself remains anonymous."* – from *Steps of Transformation* by Father Meletios Webber, an Orthodox priest

If you wish to develop your own spiritual recipe, or even if you want to move ahead without one, you need to get clear about what it is you do believe. It might be difficult if you have shut that part of your life away. But if you are serious about using the Twelve Steps for recovery, it is worth your time and energy to uncover and face what you really believe and what you really do not believe. Getting to know yourself better at this level is the only way to achieve an inner relationship with your true self.

Salt or Sugar – Identifying Your Basic Beliefs

If you are in the early stages of recovery, chances are your beliefs are murky or unsteady. Taking the time to examine what you believe can establish a foundation on which to build. By consciously knowing what you believe, you will eliminate much of the uncertainty with which many people approach life and the hundreds of decisions each of us makes every day.

The following exercises will help you focus in on what you believe. The questions are intended to point your mind in the general direction of your personal beliefs. If any question is offensive to you, don't answer it. If there are questions you can add to the list, please do so. This list of questions, and in fact this entire book, is not a rigid framework into which you should fit yourself. Rather, it is a set of options and possibilities for you to use.

EXERCISE 2-1: QUESTIONS ABOUT YOUR BELIEFS

Write a few words, a phrase or two, or a couple of brief paragraphs in response to each question. Keep your answers as clear as you can because you will be referring back to them later.

Note: If any question seems unanswerable or irritating, especially if your reaction is very strong, note it and move on.

1) What kind of thoughts come up when the word "God" is used? (For example, when used in everyday conversation, a speech, a prayer, or in a newspaper.)
2) What does the word "God" mean to you? (What definitions do you have for it, either vague or specific? What feelings does it bring up: comfort, anger, contempt, love, longing, guilt, etc.?)
3) Is there another word you prefer to use in place of the word "God"? (For example, Goddess, Universe, Self, Spirit, Lord, Nature, Great One, All There Is.)
4) If you think of yourself as an agnostic, briefly describe your core beliefs about life, including any ideas of spirituality.

5) If you think of yourself as an atheist, describe your core beliefs and disbeliefs about life, and any meaning life holds for you.
6) In your opinion, where does the idea of God come from? (For example, is it purely psychological, perhaps a reaction to our need for belonging? Is it a natural longing that is Divinely inspired? Is it a hoax perpetuated by religious groups in an attempt to control the masses?)
7) Are there existing religions or groups that have pieces of what you believe, but not the whole picture? If so, list the groups and those particular ideas.
8) Is there a particular religion to which you once belonged? If so, what prevents you from rejoining and participating?
9) If you could invent your own religion or belief system, what would it look like? (Describe its tenets and recommendations.)
10) If you have ever faced a severe crisis, did you pray, and to whom or what did you pray? What were the words you used?

Once you have completed your writing, put the information aside for at least three days. Taking a break will allow your mind to sort out what you wrote. Don't try to "process" the information; rational thought plays a very small part in clarifying spiritual ideas and beliefs. Move on to Exercise 2-2, if you wish, but do not "zip" through these exercises. If you are in a rush to "get" spirituality, take a deep breath. You may need to go a little slower than you'd like. Don't give up – just take it as it comes, without force.

EXERCISE 2-2: WATCHING FOR CLUES

Once you put an idea into your head (such as thinking about spirituality, as we're doing here), your mind will work on it in the background. As a result, you may be able to spot clues by paying attention to your dreams, daydreams, random thoughts, or even the songs you are unconsciously singing or humming.

If you usually remember the dreams you have at night, scan them for possible messages about your spiritual ideas. If you do not tend to remember your dreams, but are interested in doing so, try telling yourself, just before going to sleep, that you wish to remember your dreams. As soon as you wake up, write the dreams down before they escape your memory. As you write, use your own words to describe the dream; include feelings, thoughts, images, and other impressions. Later in the day, reread them. You may be surprised at how obvious the messages are. You may also want to get further insight by consulting some of the excellent books about interpreting dreams, but usually your own interpretations are the most reliable and revealing.

If you spend quiet time or meditation time, notice what your mind is telling you, but avoid deliberately focusing on this subject. In other words, where at all possible, simply observe.

As you move through the day, if you find yourself singing a song or humming a tune, take a look at the words and also look at your own memories related to that song.

After a few days of consciously observing your thoughts, proceed to the next section, where you'll be taking another look at what you wrote in Exercise 2-1.

Yesterday and Today – Identifying Stale Ideas and Old Favorites

Depending on several factors, such as how you were raised, the community in which you lived growing up, the one in which you live now, and the people and ideas to which you were and are most often exposed, you may have strong ideas about God, whether positive, negative, or both. Some of these ideas are "leftovers" and are no longer true for you. This next exercise will help you sort through what to keep and what to consider throwing away.

EXERCISE 2-3: MINING FOR WHAT'S TRUE

To bring yourself up to date – to clarify what is really true for you today – gather the answers you wrote in Exercise 2-1, and apply the following steps:

1) For each response, ask yourself if this is what you used to believe or whether it's what you really do believe now. (If you don't know, or cannot do this step, just go on to the remainder of the steps in this exercise.)

2) Using the list you compiled in Exercise 2-1, sort out the items according to the reaction they caused. For example: if you felt guilt, anger, elation, or confusion, list each of those feelings along the left side of a piece of paper, and briefly list the related items beside the reaction they bring up, as shown below.

Example: Listing Reactions and Triggers

Feeling/Reaction	Reaction Trigger
Guilt	Church attendance; Confession
Anger	Catholic Church; mortal sin; punishment in hell; only Jesus can save us
Happiness/Hope	Life after death; forgiveness; "May the Force Be With You" in the Star Wars movie.
Confusion	The Pope's infallibility; going to hell for getting a divorce; birth control or abortion; agnosticism; God as the opiate of the masses?; who gets to go to heaven?; is heaven literally a place?; what does it really mean to be a Catholic or a Christian? "gender" of God
Comfort	Being in nature; Let the Mystery Be; loving God; nonjudgmental God

3) For each part of the list you made in this exercise, as you review each item in the list, consider the reaction or feeling it brought up, and with that in mind, decide whether you want to:

   a) include that idea as part of your life.

   b) completely discard it from your life.

c) consider whether it might be useful to you in some way, perhaps in a different setting or with some changes.
4) Now that you have sorted through your beliefs, take one more look through the eyes of what is true for you today (as opposed to what you used to believe). Be especially alert for those areas in which you had a strong reaction, either positive or negative.

That Which You Seek – Identifying What's Spiritual

Before doing any more work on spirituality, stop and be sure you know the difference between spirituality and intellectual knowledge. For example, while you may be willing to believe that the Ten Commandments are good rules, it's an entirely different matter to have them fit for you in terms of your own personal way of seeing the world. While many people would quickly agree that the Ten Commandments are a good standard for morality and religion, some of those people believe that killing another person for any reason is against their moral code, while others may believe that their religious ideas are worth killing for.

This book does not encourage you to grab a standard package of religious or spiritual ideas before you have decided what they really mean to you at a deeper level. After all, recovery is often a matter of life and death. If spirituality is the core concept of Twelve-Step recovery, it is important to pay close attention to how you frame your own personal spiritual ideas.

EXERCISE 2-4: A FEW MORE QUESTIONS

The previous exercises focused on the way you describe or label God, religion, or spirituality in light of how you fit with existing cultural ideas. The questions in this exercise are more about your "gut-level" experiences or ideas, without the trappings of organized thought. Feel free to use these questions to shake loose any ideas that may not have surfaced in earlier exercises.

1) Have you ever had a "sacred" experience (for example, felt filled up when looking at a rainbow or walking in a place of natural beauty, or witnessed the birth of a child, or were touched by a feeling of deep love or unselfishness)?

2) Have you ever had a feeling of overwhelming comfort or peace? If so, recall the details, where, when, etc.?

3) Is there a particular person that makes more sense to you than most others do? If so, what is it about them that makes them that way for you?

4) If you could have personal self-satisfaction, what would that look and feel like?

5) Imagine you are on a planet that has never heard of spirituality. How would you explain it to the beings who live there?

There are no right or wrong answers. Just be open to the possibility that your own answers will reveal additional information to you about what you really believe on a spiritual level.

Shortcuts – Jumping to Vague Conclusions

It may be that, rather than not knowing what you believe, you are disturbed by an inability to clearly define what you believe. This can be a huge obstacle in the search for a meaningful belief system. For example, you may already believe that God is "love," but you aren't really sure your idea would hold up if challenged. Using another example, you may believe in reincarnation, but you can't explain how it works or even why you believe it.

We live in a world that expects us to justify and explain ourselves. But in matters of personal philosophy or spirituality, it may not be desirable or even realistic to have such expectations of ourselves and others. When an idea or concept fails to lend itself to rational explanation, it does not mean the idea has no merit. It simply means that the concept cannot be defined logically based on what our limited thinking can comprehend.

Healthy Uncertainty

The inability to define spiritual or philosophical ideas in great detail is not only normal, it is psychologically sound. Many of the common ideas that thread our lives together are not clearly defined.

Gravity and electricity are good examples, as mentioned in an earlier chapter. Most of us believe that gravity is what keeps us on the ground, but how many can prove it or go into detail about how it works? For most of us, our interaction with electricity is another example of a power that we enjoy but cannot explain. In fact, our interactions with gravity and electricity are excellent illustrations of the way each of us employs faith at some level every day. We do not see gravity or electricity, yet we rely on them. No proof is needed, yet we often place our lives in their care, trusting they are real.

Acceptance Without Gullibility

Unless you are in a position to devote most or all of your time to scientific study, you need to accept much of what you believe on the basis of personal experience and discernment. This is especially true of spiritual and philosophical matters. It is just not possible to prove or disprove on a logical basis much of what we believe. And in fact, the reverse may be true: When someone believes that they know what you *should* believe, especially if they are ready to explain the reasons, you should probably run away as fast as you can. You are the only one who knows what feels right and true to you. No one can define it for you.

Clarifying your beliefs essentially means taking an inventory of what you believe and then asking yourself whether those beliefs are current with your existing values. You do not need to be able to describe the mechanics of your beliefs or to argue their merits. Based on discussion and feedback from many people now in Twelve-Step programs, the best way to know what you believe spiritually is by going with your intuition or your inner voice. When something "rings true" for you, that is enough. No need to explain, and you are free to change what you believe at any time.

ϒϒϒ

> *"It may be possible to find explanations of spiritual experiences such as ours, but I have often tried to explain my own and have succeeded only in giving the story of it. I know the feeling it gave me and the results it has brought, but I realize I may never fully understand its deeper why and how."*
> – from *As Bill Sees It*

Chapter Three

CREATING YOUR RECIPE

"What is in a name? That which we call a rose by any other name would smell as sweet."
– William Shakespeare,
Romeo and Juliet, 1593-1596

Once you have used the ideas in Chapter 2 to clarify the components of what you believe, you can work with that information to better define your spiritual recipe. This recipe can be anything you want it to be. It can be your own version of atheism or agnosticism, your personal set of unique ideas, or a blend of various elements from one or more ideologies or established religions. By pulling these ingredients together, you will then have a recipe to use as you move through recovery. You can also decide whether to give your recipe a name. It's up to you. For many people, a name is a helpful kind of shorthand, while for others, a name can be restrictive or smothering.

Perusing Existing Recipes for Ideas

Start the process of finalizing your own spiritual recipe by comparing your beliefs with some existing world religions and philosophies. While there are many excellent resources for doing so, this section provides a brief overview of several of these religions and philosophies. To follow up on or get more information about one or more world religions, see the listing of books and websites in *Resources* in the back of this book.

According to several of the texts about world religions, the major religions fall into the following seven groups: Judaism, Christianity, Islam, and the Eastern religions of Hinduism, Buddhism, Confucianism, and Taoism.

The idea of a personal God (a personality, usually masculine) is primarily confined to **Judaism**, **Christianity**, and **Islam**, and is what most people in the Western World think of when the word religion is used. Among each of these groups, there are thousands of variations. Just as many new Twelve-Step recovery groups have started with "a resentment and a coffee pot," the same principle seems to apply to religion. **Christianity** originated with Catholicism, which carried over many of the precepts of **Judaism**. The Protestant (as in *protest*) churches, were then formed by people who saw a need to vary from the Catholic Church. There are now many versions of Christianity, including the Eastern Orthodox,

Calvinist, Lutheran, Presbyterian, Anglican, Episcopal, Baptist, Quaker, Mormon, Church of Christ, Christian Science, Religious Science, Divine Science, Evangelical, Methodist, Unity, Pentecostal, Gnosticism, and Messianic Judaism Churches. This is not a comprehensive list. Among these, there are many variations and offshoots! **Islam**, while it includes Jesus as one of its prophets, believes in one God, but is not Christian because it does not name Jesus as God, as the Christian churches do.

The **Eastern religions** do not have the same emphasis on God, but believe that the universe itself is God or part of God, or that God is comprised of a group of lesser gods. God is not a "personality" in these religions, although there are gods with various personality traits. Primarily, however, the Eastern religions focus more on individual spiritual development or practices rather than on deity worship.

Apart from the major religions, **other ideologies** include Paganism (Wicca, Witchcraft, Goddess Worship, Druidism, and Norse Paganism), Native American Spirituality, World Pantheism (nature worship), Scientology, agnosticism, and atheism. And even atheism includes religious organizations. There is no belief in a deity in either Buddhism or Unitarian Universalism, for example, and these are sometimes classified as atheist groups.

Belief in God is not the only factor in sorting through spiritual ideas. The *practices* of various groups and religions are also significant. For example, Yoga, which many Westerners consider a form of physical conditioning, is a word that means "spiritual practice." Yoga originated with Hinduism as a way to spiritual enlightenment. Other spiritual practices include fasting, prayer, dancing, confession, flagellation, whirling, dietary restrictions, evangelism, self-imposed poverty, charitable giving, sexual abstinence, and just about anything else people have tried in the pursuit of spiritual connection or religion.

No matter what you do or do not believe, you are likely to learn something surprising if you start exploring. If you have computer access to the Internet, research is especially easy. Just by entering one word – for example, atheism – you may find thousands of links to follow in any number of directions. Some of the information will be serious and focused, and at the other end of the spectrum, some will be lighthearted and fun. See the next section for some examples of what you might find as you roam the World Wide Web.

Multiple Choice Taste-Testing

One of my favorite Internet sites is www.belief.net. This site provides links, articles, discussion, meditations, and general information about almost any ideology you can name.

A sampling of the website's offerings on one particular day included articles about, and links to, the following topics:
- Questioning whether or not God controls the American presidency
- The current political silence of real Christianity
- Contents of an American Indian museum
- Anglicans launching a diplomatic push

- A suggestion that South Park is TV's best religion show
- Information about Kabbalah weddings
- Articles about angels and guides, deism vs. theism, gender and sexuality
- A flash presentation of readers' prayers for troops in Iraq

The site also includes questionnaires, such as "What's Your Spiritual Type," "Find Your Spiritual Path," and "Belief-O-Matic™," which are all playful while offering valuable insight into your compatibility with existing ideas or world religions or philosophies. As the tongue-in-cheek warning states, "Belief-O-Matic™ assumes no legal liability for the ultimate fate of your soul."

There are many other websites devoted to spiritual seeking and information, some of which are listed in *Resources* near the back of this book. You can also try entering a few words and phrases to see what comes up; for example, spirituality, spiritual path, atheism, agnosticism, or whatever you are curious about. Of course, the quality and credibility of the sites vary widely, but that's what searching is all about – you get to decide for yourself what is worthwhile reading.

Whether you take the sites seriously or in fun, you will probably learn about a few new ideologies, and in the process, you may find yourself questioning your own from a new perspective.

Mix and Match – Creating Your Own Spiritual Blend

If you were ever told what to believe or how to fit in with a church or other institution, you have every reason to back away from "organized" ideas. This short story about the topic of organized religion says it best. God and the Devil are walking side-by-side, when God stoops over to pick up something from the ground. "What is it?" the Devil asks. "It's Truth," God replies, to which the Devil responds, "Here, let me have it and I'll organize it for you."

While many existing religions and other groups might appeal to you in some ways, you do not need to be locked into one particular way or practice. Try different combinations until you find what fits for you.

If you have some idea of the components of your ideology – for example, if you like practicing Zen meditation, yet you wish to enjoy the "smells and the bells" of Catholicism or a similar religion – you are encouraged to create your own "spiritual recipe." This exercise is especially useful if you have access to the Internet.

EXERCISE 3-1: GATHERING THE INGREDIENTS

By now, you have identified some of the ingredients that comprise your spiritual recipe. In this exercise, you'll make a list of the ideas and practices that fit best for you. This allows you to create a cohesive picture of your personal spiritual tastes and look at whether they can be aligned with or reinforced by existing ideologies.

1) Get two 8-1/2 x 11 inch pieces of paper and draw a line down the middle of each. Label one page "Beliefs," and the second page "Practices."

2) In the first column of the "Beliefs" page, list the ideas you have found so far that are closest to your own beliefs about spirituality. Be as specific as possible. For example, if you think there is power in gathering as a community, list "power of community" or "power of group prayer" or "power of community service" as a component of your spirituality. If you are leaning toward certain aspects of Christianity, list those aspects specifically, such as "the Holy Trinity" or "Heaven and Hell." If you are an atheist, be specific about the details, "natural law is all there is," or "the human mind creates reality."

Example: Completed "Beliefs" Page

Beliefs	
The Universe is One	
Human beings are all part of that One	
Natural law is sacred	
Intuition is a natural talent and can help us develop spiritually	
When we die, our energy returns to the great body of energy that is the Universe	
Following conscience is the only morality we need	
When we put out a clear intention, the Universe provides	
Our primary purpose is to evolve as part of the Universal Creativity	

3) In the first column of the "Practices" page, list the activities or actions that fit best for you in terms of creating or strengthening inner connection. For example, if you find that walking in nature has special meaning for you, list that. Maybe meditation, or running, or playing sacred music are what make you feel most at peace with yourself. Again, be as specific as possible.

Example: Completed "Practices" Page

Practices	
Meditation	
Acceptance of all that is	
Group prayer	
Dancing to replace "thinking" with "being"	
Hiking	
Sacred music/Gregorian Chant	
Vegetarianism	
Pacifism	
Honoring all life as sacred	

4) Do some research: Enter the terms from both pages as search items on the Internet (at home, your local library, or some other source of computer access) and "follow the paths." For example, during one search of "meditation," the results included chanting, mountain hiking, Taoism, and other references.

During your search, do the following three things:

- In the right-hand column of each page, write down the names of any groups or website addresses that match your list items, and if possible, print out website pages that are of special interest.

- If you find other items that belong in the first column of either page, add them.
- Roam the Internet, following links and entering new search words.

Do as much research as interests you (a few minutes, hours, or spread out over a longer period of time).

Example: 20-Minute Search Session Results

Beliefs	
The Universe is One	God = Universe; Pantheism, Taoism, but not atheism. Pantheism people = Eckhart, Spinoza, Whitman, Plato, Sagan, Emerson.
Human beings are all part of that One	Pantheism (Universe is all there is, ultimate reality, we are part of it.)
Natural law is sacred	Universe is sacred (Pantheism)
Intuition is a natural talent and can help us develop spiritually	Intuition as "natural" - Pantheism
When we die, our energy returns to the great body of energy that is the Universe	Definitely Pantheism; Taoism?
Following conscience is the only morality we need	Pantheism (again!); natural law = Divine law
When we put out a clear intention, the Universe provides	Religious Science; Pantheism; others
Our primary purpose is to evolve as part of the Universal Creativity	Pantheism; Taoism; maybe Atheism

Practices	
Meditation	Hinduism, all Eastern religions, Different forms; hiking as meditation = Pantheism
Acceptance of all that is.	Taoism; Pantheism
Group prayer	Everybody, at least so far today on the Internet
Dancing to replace "thinking" with "being"	Sufism; but dancing part of lots of groups, incl. Native American, Judaism, others
Hiking	See meditation. Tibet/Nepal (Hinduism and Buddhism)
Sacred music/Gregorian Chant	Greg Chant = Catholicism; also Buddhism (see World Festival of Sacred Music; started by Dalai Lama)
Vegetarianism	Buddhism, members of some Christian groups, Hindus, Hare Krishna, Sikh, Jain; Choctaw Indians (corn is Divine; melons in heaven!);
Pacifism	Buddhism (no killing); Quakers; Mennonites; Unitarian Universalism; Thoreau, Gandhi
Honoring all life as sacred	Anti-abortionists; just about all religions

Take as much time as you like, then proceed to Exercise 3-2.

———————

Exercise 3-2: Zeroing in on Your Overall Package

After you have completed Exercise 3-1, focus on the results you listed in the right-hand column of each page.

1) Identify any instances of repeated search results. For example, the sample results from Exercise 3-1 show instances of Taoism and other religions, but the concept of Pantheism is repeated in several places.

2) Take the items identified in step 1 and do some more digging, either on the Internet, a bookstore, or at the library.

By the time you are done with this exercise, you will see which existing ideologies, if any, fit with what you already believe. The major goal is to be clearer about what you believe.

Exercise 3-3: Naming Your Spiritual Recipe

This exercise isn't designed to create limitations or fixed ideas by pasting labels on your spiritual ideas. However, a name or a phrase for your personal spirituality can make it more accessible when you are working with the Twelve Steps. It is not necessary to do this, but if you do, it will make life easier later on.

1) Give a name to your personal spiritual recipe. As you do this, bear in mind that naming can be a very powerful exercise. Some cultures consider naming to be a sacred act, one that imparts an energy to the person or object being named, depending on the

meaning and nature of the name itself. If you are satisfied with a label that already exists, such as Pantheism in the previous example, then use it. If you feel it would be restrictive to use an existing label, create a new one. Choose a name that will clearly represent your spiritual recipe, as clearly as the word meatloaf makes you think of a meat-flavored casserole. Over time, your mind will not need to process through each "ingredient," but will identify with the feelings and intentions of the whole package. Have some fun. You could be a "Zen Judaist," an "Earth-Loving Tree Hugger" or a "Nonviolent Atheist"! It's up to you.

2) Write the word or phrase down on a piece of paper and put it in a special place. It represents your personal Truth, and holds the intentions of Integrity and Purpose.

Fine Dining – Applying Your Recipe to the Steps

Now that you have clarified and perhaps named your spirituality, take a closer look at how it fits with the Twelve Steps. Below is another copy of the Twelve Steps for easy reference.

1. We admitted we were powerless over alcohol – that our lives had become unmanageable.
2. Came to believe that a **Power greater than ourselves** could restore us to sanity.
3. Made a decision to turn our will and our lives over to the care of **God** as we understood **Him**.
4. Made a searching and fearless moral inventory of ourselves.

5. Admitted to **God**, to ourselves, and to another human being the exact nature of our wrongs.
6. Were entirely ready to have **God** remove all these defects of character.
7. Humbly asked **Him** to remove our shortcomings.
8. Made a list of all persons we had harmed, and became willing to make amends to them all.
9. Made direct amends to such people wherever possible, except when to do so would injure them or others.
10. Continued to take personal inventory and when we were wrong promptly admitted it.
11. Sought through prayer and meditation to improve our conscious contact with **God**, as we understood **Him**, praying only for knowledge of **His** will for us and the power to carry that out.
12. Having had a spiritual awakening as the result of these Steps, we tried to carry this message to alcoholics, and to practice these principles in all our affairs.

Copyright © A.A. World Services, Inc.

Along with your newly gathered spiritual ideas, use the following exercises to apply them to the Steps. Make your best attempt to try each of these exercises at least once.

Exercise 3-4: Naming the Focal Point of Your Spiritual Recipe

This exercise will help you create a word or phrase to replace or add to the word "God" in the Twelve Steps.

1) Briefly recall what the word "God" or "Higher Power" appeared to mean when you last read the Twelve Steps. (Reread them if you need to refresh your memory.)

2) Now read through the Steps, but this time, focus or keep in mind the spiritual recipe you have assembled.
3) For each reference to God in those Steps (Power Great Than Ourselves, God, Him), replace that idea with the highest principle of your spiritual recipe. If you do not have a specific word or phrase in mind, you can use something less specific, such as "the Essence of My Highest Personal Beliefs."

EXERCISE 3-5: READING THE STEPS WITH NEW EYES

This exercise uses the word or phrase you created in Exercise 3-4.

1) Write the word or phrase you substituted for "God" in the previous exercise.
2) Read through all Twelve Steps, and when the word God appears, use it, but internally translate its meaning. For example, as you read Step Two, "Came to believe that a *Power greater than ourselves* could restore us to sanity," leave the words as they are, but think about your own spiritual beliefs as you do so. When you say, "a Power greater than ourselves," let this Power be whatever you decide it is by silently thinking about its meaning.

By now, I hope you have begun to feel comfortable thinking about God in the Twelve Steps in your own way. *The key to using the Steps is really the willingness to put your fears, closed-mindedness, and resistance aside, and to know that you are absolutely free to believe as you wish.* If you are still finding yourself stuck or repelled by spirituality or references to God, please keep reading. The next chapter directly addresses these roadblocks.

Chapter Four

Going Meatless – When God Doesn't Fit

"It is the rare alcoholic who accepts the 'higher power' malarkey without any quibbling."
— Katherine Ketcham and William F. Asbury,
Beyond the Influence: Understanding and Defeating Alcoholism (New York: Bantam Books, 2000).

If you are deeply grounded in atheism, worried about your agnosticism, blocked by anger, or feeling isolated by your unique spirituality, you are not doomed to fail at using the Twelve Steps. There is a place at the table for everyone in the Twelve-Step programs, and you are the only one who can decide whether it fits for you.

Disbelief – Using the Steps as an Atheist Without Losing Integrity

If you are an entrenched atheist (that is, you strongly believe that no God exists), you have probably listened to every argument, all the best reasons for surrendering yourself to a higher power, and you are still not convinced. Yet here you are, willing enough (or desperate enough) to continue looking for a way to use the Twelve Steps while remaining true to yourself. There's no guarantee that you will resolve your difficulty, but your willingness to stay open to new ideas means you have an excellent chance of using the Twelve Steps to make your life better.

Contrary to what some people believe, the Twelve-Step programs are not attempting to convert anyone. Part of Tradition Eleven of Alcoholics Anonymous states, "Our public relations policy is based on attraction rather than promotion." While AA is a frequent target of criticism (there are numerous websites that rabidly oppose AA, such as www.positiveatheism.org), the organization itself "neither endorses nor opposes any causes." Oddly enough, AA (and to my knowledge, every other Twelve-Step group) does not even attempt to respond to its attackers. Everyone is welcome; no one is refused (unless they are violent or deliberately disrupting a meeting); and the only requirement for membership is a desire to stop drinking (or for other groups, a desire to stop the self-destructive behavior). AA cannot prevent or control the behaviors of its individual members, but it encourages anonymity so that *nobody has the authority to define or represent the organization or its principles.*

As **Andrea** relates, "In more than twenty years of personal experience, I have never been told I need to believe or do anything, and I have never seen anyone else forced to believe or do anything."

"Take what you like and leave the rest" is frequently stated at many meetings. If you have been warned about religious proselytizing, evaluate the situation for yourself. You will not be 'tricked" into staying, nor forced to believe or to take any actions. It may, however, save your life.

At the risk of repeating some basic information, here is a reminder: Twelve-Step recovery is a spiritual program, but you do *not* need to believe in God or be affiliated with any religion to use the Steps for recovery. If anyone tells you otherwise, they are acting in opposition to the principles of the Twelve Steps. Just find someone else to talk to. Check out a few meetings, look around for people similar to yourself, and notice the way we all seem to support each other. For many atheists, that support is the real power.

ΥΥΥ

"While mainstream media often implies that 'religious' and 'spiritual' are synonymous, Simon believes that 'religion' reflects the teachings of particular organized religions that, in general, present specific rules, regulations, and rituals that must be followed in order to experience a connection with the Divine,

usually represented as a Supreme (male) Being outside of humanity. On the other hand, 'spirituality' generally entails a more personal, inner-directed, and individual experience of the Divine, which is represented as an integral aspect of our own humanity. – Hollywood Producer Stephen Simon, from *The Force Is with You: Mystical Movie Messages That Inspire Our Lives*, 2002.

If you do encounter people who try to convince you that you need God, please remember that they are acting as individuals, and are not speaking with any kind of authority. If possible, accept their arguments gracefully (remember that *love and tolerance is our code*). They are mistaken in their well-meaning efforts. It's only human to want to convince others of what we believe has relieved us of our pain. While it is unfair to expect someone new to fend for themselves, there are no rules that prevent people from saying whatever they want to say. This often causes problems, but overall, it is a small price to pay for maintaining equality among members.

Although being an atheist might seem to make Twelve-Step recovery especially difficult or might seem to be asking you to be hypocritical, keep in mind that you are not the first atheist to land in recovery. There were some atheists and agnostics present when the original Twelve Steps were written, and their input created a spiritual loophole for you. If you are open-minded enough to overlook the constant use of the word God and the references to it, the Steps will work for you, as they have for many others that believe as you do.

Jeremy is one atheist who was initially put off by the idea of spirituality, but who came to see that he could use his own concepts, with no need to make excuses to anyone:

"I came into the Program hoping to get help, but was really discouraged when I heard it was a spiritual program. In the past, this has usually meant some kind of deity worship. I had discarded that concept in my early teens, figuring that if God exists and is such a wonderful being, I won't roast in hell just for being true to myself. I was not willing to pay homage to something or someone just to keep myself out of trouble."

"The ideas in the Program were reasonable, but the prayer thing, especially at the end of a meeting, was really tough. If I hadn't been so desperate, I would have left during the first week. But I *was* desperate; I knew this was my last stop. So my big challenge was to try it out without lying to myself or anyone else."

"A few weeks into the Program, I figured out that I needed a sponsor, and that's when I had to face the whole idea of what to do about my different beliefs. I didn't know whether I'd get fired or lectured, but I asked Ray because he seemed to have his feet on the ground and to be caring about people. I had no idea how he felt about religion, so I was relieved when he said my atheism didn't matter. He did ask me to pray, but suggested that I go through the motions, and not pray *to* anyone or anything. I did it more as an exercise in psychology. I was surprised to find it made me feel quieter and steadier, so I kept doing it."

"Even so, I hated it when people talked about God saving them, doing something good for them, or testing them, like there was a *personality* involved. I took someone's suggestion to substitute 'the power of the group' in place of God, and it works well for me. For the most part, having a way to deal with the God thing has taken the sting out of it."

"I've read a little bit about the history of AA, which is where it all started, and how there were atheists right from the beginning. I'm not sure how many of them stayed sober, but I'm still clean after seven years, and I still have my values and my beliefs. I am not so judgmental as I was about people who believe that their God is the only way to go. Whatever they want to believe doesn't matter to me, especially in recovery. We're all just doing the best we know how."

EXERCISE 4-1: SEARCHING FOR THE WORDS

There are many names and concepts you can use in place of "God" or "Higher Power," such as Good Orderly Direction (GOD), Love, the Universe, and All There Is. Check out the following exercise if you'd like help choosing a good replacement. This is similar to some of the exercises in Chapter 3, but rather than naming the whole spiritual recipe, you will be choosing a specific word or phrase to use in place of "God" or "Higher Power."

Review the information you gathered in earlier exercises. You may find the word or phrase without working very hard at it. If you created a name for your spiritual recipe, consider finding a word that captures the essence of that package. For example, if you are a "tree hugger," it could be "Tree Essence."

If the previous step in this exercise doesn't work for you, make a list of things over which you have no control, such as nature in general, or the ocean, sun, moon, gravity, or other forces. See if any of those would serve as a good name.

Imagine describing your atheism to someone else and pay close attention to the words you use.

If you are still unable to come up with anything, just use the words "I don't know" or "to be determined" as a placeholder. You can change it later, if you wish.

Confusion and Uncertainty – The Advantage of Agnosticism in Using the Steps

Agnosticism (that is, you neither believe nor disbelieve in God) might be the easiest philosophy from which to approach Twelve-Step recovery, since, in most cases, it carries the fewest number of preconceived ideas. As an agnostic, you are neither set on a particular religious stance, nor are you completely closed to the idea of spirituality. Even if you are dead set against religion, for the purposes of recovery, you might still be better off than someone who is determined to hold onto old beliefs.

Glenn talks of being wary about religion, specifically Christianity, until he found the spirituality in Twelve-Step recovery:

"I have found it true that Narcotics Anonymous is a spiritual, not a religious program. I am thankful for that. When I went to treatment, I didn't want to hear about religion. If I had, I would have gone to Church. Very few addicts, when their addiction has them firmly in their grasp, want to hear about the Bible, or Jesus Christ, or other subjects with religious overtones."

"Many addicts feel that God has let them down, and aren't too happy with Him. Many are ashamed to face Him. The best advice that I received in treatment was to throw everything I had ever learned about God in the trash, and start over. And, thank God, I did. I trashed all that stuff about God being a punishing and vengeful God. I especially trashed what 'religious' people told me when they said, 'Just pray and ask Jesus to take away your urge to use and drink, and He will,' because I knew from personal experience that it wasn't true. If it was, all addicts and alcoholics would eventually be cured. How many of us haven't said the 'Drunk's Prayer' (*If you help me this time, I'll never do this again*) while hovering over a toilet, or laying in a ditch? And how can anyone say that the Drunk's Prayer isn't said in sincerity? When you think you're going to die, you get *really* sincere. Addiction, and God, are just not that simple."

Whether or not you agree with Glenn's outlook, his idea about "trashing all that stuff about God" worked well for him. Clearing the religious and spiritual slate is one way to discover and fully embrace your own beliefs.

ᛘᛘᛘ

"Sometimes A.A. comes harder to those who have lost or rejected faith than to those who never had any faith at all, for they think they have tried faith and found it wanting. They have tried the way of faith and the way of no faith."
– from *Twelve Steps and Twelve Traditions*

EXERCISE 4-2: USING THE BIG BOOK

Read "We Agnostics" in the book *Alcoholics Anonymous,* and then do the following:

1) Note which parts of the chapter make sense and which do not.
2) Talk to people about those specific confusions.
3) Listen in meetings for others who have had similar confusions, and talk to them about how they are developing their spirituality.

If you have abandoned a religious faith from an earlier time in your life, take a close look at whether some of those ideas are still shadowing you. Sometimes your conscious mind can say one thing, but your unconscious mind remains influenced by the past. It is impossible to relax and trust in the direction of your life if an old God is ready to cast you into the depths of hell! Review the information you gathered in the exercises in Chapters 2 and 3 earlier in this book (or do the exercises if you haven't yet done them) and look for ways in which the past is affecting your present views on spirituality.

If you really are not decided about where you stand with the God thing, you can invent a spiritual recipe that does not define God in any way. And if you really cannot come up with anything right now, don't force it.

The whole point of finding or creating a spiritual recipe for yourself is to find peace and comfort from within.

Armed and Wary – Approaching Spirituality from Anger and Distrust

When you are angry with God, or even with a Church that represents God, your anger may be detracting from what recovery offers – the feeling of being comfortable with yourself and others, of belonging, of being able to love and be loved. These outcomes are the direct result of finding and applying spirituality to your life. If you are stuck in anger, you need to make a choice: Be willing to open up to God about your anger, or find a new God or a new spiritual approach.

ɤɤɤ

> *"Holding on to anger is like grasping a hot coal with the intent of throwing it at someone else; you are the one getting burned."* – Buddha

Even if you can live with your own anger, it probably interferes with the benefits of being in a group of other recovering people, which is a key component of recovery. Unless you have a very good reason for holding on to your anger, unless it provides clear and tangible benefits, please consider finding a way to let go of it or alleviate it. Many people come into recovery with so much anger that they are afraid they will be completely overcome by it, and either implode or explode. But like any other bottled up emotion, it screams to get out. The more you hold it in, the harder it pushes, and the more energy you need to use to keep it under control. It can harm you physically, as well as mentally, emotionally, and spiritually.

One specific effect of anger is that it tends to push other people away. Even when you hold it in or hide it, anger has its own invisible energy that other people detect and avoid, either consciously or unconsciously. In Twelve-Step recovery, this can be detrimental because much of our success comes from interacting with other recovering people. We share thoughts and feelings with each other, and even without knowing why this works so well, we know from experience that it does make a difference. We need each other in recovery, and if your anger keeps you from fully interacting with others, you would be wise to look at ways of letting it go.

ϓϓϓ

> *"To watch people recover, to see them help others, to watch loneliness vanish, to see a fellowship grow up about you, to have a host of friends – this is an experience you must not miss. We know you will not want to miss it. Frequent contact with newcomers and with each other is the bright spot of our lives."*
> – from *Alcoholics Anonymous*

EXERCISE 4-3: ACCEPTING ANGER

Set aside 15 or 20 minutes for this exercise, and find a comfortable position in which to sit. Read through the entire exercise before beginning, so that you can create the scene in your mind. (You could also choose to make a recording of this exercise for yourself, which will allow you to go even deeper into this guided meditation.)

Breathe slowly and deeply, and with each breath, relax a little more each time as you count down from ten to one by saying internally, "Breathe in, ten ten ten, breathe out, ten ten ten. Breathe in nine nine nine, breathe out, nine nine nine," and continue on until you have finished with the number one.

Now picture a quiet forest, thick with large pine trees. You are walking on a thick cushion of pine needles that have fallen for hundreds of years. There are green ferns just a few feet away, and birds flitting about in the trees. As you look up through the highest branches, you can see the sky, a strong, rich blue with a few puffy white clouds barely moving along.

A gentle being appears, someone obviously safe and trustworthy, and you are curious about the large box they are watching. As you walk over to the box, you see it is filled with writhing snakes trying to escape.

The gentle being speaks quietly, "Have you ever seen such angry creatures?" and you can see that the snakes are really unhappy about being penned in. The gentle being then beckons you to watch as one of the sides is removed from the box. The snakes frantically slither off into the forest, and within moments, the only sound is an occasional rustle of leaves in the distance. "Quiet now, isn't it? They hate being boxed up. When they're free to move individually, they are not much of a threat. " The gentle being and the box disappear, and you are left to consider what just happened.

Now think about your own anger and how much easier it would be if you could just notice it and let it be part of your own forest, your life. And also notice that, when each spark of anger occurs, you can consciously decide not to keep it locked up. You can accept and then release it, without acting it out. Just notice the feeling of anger as you would notice a bird flying by. You can notice that it's there, and you can watch it move through your mind and then out again. It's safe to do this.

The danger of being hurtful to yourself or to others is greatly reduced. This feeling of accepting anger also means that other feelings have an equal chance of being noticed and felt. Instead of a storage place for anger, you now have room for warmth and caring, fun and happiness, and love for yourself and others.

Picture yourself feeling safe and filled with self-respect, knowing that you can act with good intentions and love whenever you choose to do so. And feel what it's like to have that self-respect, to know that you are a really wonderful person that knows how to feel anger without having to act outwardly or implode internally.

Enjoy that feeling for a few minutes, then take a few long, deep breaths. Very gradually, begin to notice how your body feels. Move your toes and your fingers. Now move your arms and legs, and slowly open your eyes. Take a few minutes to savor the feeling of safety, and try to carry it with you as move into the rest of your day.

Acceptance is one way to deal with anger. If shame is keeping you from opening up your anger, it will not go away by itself. It festers and boils until it comes to the surface, either directly or indirectly. By applying the Twelve Steps to your anger, you can replace anger with serenity and self-respect. By being honest with yourself about your level of anger, and by using the Steps to the best of your ability, you can be happy, joyous, and free.

Paula's story is about overcoming anger and resentment, and finding a spirituality that did not ask her to see herself as defective because of her sexual preferences: "I was always searching for something greater than myself. I somehow knew it existed, even during the years when two of the local women hauled me off to Sunday school at the Presbyterian Church down the street. I was pressured and shamed into learning the Books of the Bible. And that was my introduction to religion, so why would I want to do more of the same? I decided I didn't."

"Later, at 14 or 15, I was still actively searching. My older sister invited me to join her at another Presbyterian church in town, and I liked being with her, so I went. I joined a group of my sister's friends, and we wrote a play called 'Walking for the Lord.' We had a great time with the production, as we walked toward the front of the church saying, 'We are walking for the Lord.' I laugh a little about it now, but at the time, it really meant a lot to me."

"At church, they said it was a sin to be a homosexual. I had long been attracted to girls and women, as well as to boys. As my sexuality developed, I realized that my attraction to women was stronger. I asked myself, 'If God created me, why would being who I am be a sin?' It was very hard to make it all fit. Not surprisingly,

I copped a resentment, first with the Church itself, and eventually, with the churchgoers, who were constantly trying to cram their ideas into my brain. I was afraid to talk to any clergy about any of this, fearing that if I did, they'd try to change me. I knew I didn't need to be 'healed.' "

"When I arrived in AA and noticed it included God, one of my first thoughts was 'Oh, no – not again! Are these people going to turn against me because I'm gay?' I wanted so much to be in a group of people who were searching and who had open minds, but my internal struggle had held me back from really jumping into the Program with an open heart and mind. Eventually, as I worked the Twelve Steps with a sponsor over the next year and a half, I really got it that they were saying 'God, as we understood Him.' It was huge for me – like I was given a giant potpourri basket filled with various ideas, and I could choose any combination to make my own spirituality. I also realized that spirituality is not the same as religion, and that spirituality is what I had been looking for all along."

"Now I find peace and solace in the spiritual aspects of this Program because I was able to find a God of my understanding. Especially when I am out in nature or by the ocean, I can really grasp that there is something greater than myself. And over time, my resentments towards the Church and God have dissipated. After I had been in recovery for a while, I went to a Unitarian Church and it seemed to fit the spirituality I felt in AA: more inclusive rather than exclusive."

"The Twelve Steps, and in particular, AA, have opened the door to a spirituality that is mine, and now I have found a place in which I belong, and in which I am accepted for who I am. I feel so grateful."

Unique Beliefs – Working with a Sponsor Who Has a Different Spiritual Recipe

An ideal sponsor has the attitude and values that you would like to have, including the same spiritual recipe. But that's the ideal. It's rare to find a sponsor relationship in which *all* the pieces fit perfectly.

If you have been looking for a sponsor, but cannot find someone who is on a spiritual path that is closely aligned with yours, or if you already have a sponsor with different spiritual ideas than your own, you can still have a mutually supportive relationship. As with any relationship, you need to put time and care into it so that it meets both your needs.

One tool that works well in sponsor/sponsee relationships is to "Take What You Like and Leave the Rest." Focus on your common values, starting with the goal of being successful in recovery. Focus on your similarities rather than your differences, remembering why you chose that person for your sponsor in the first place.

If you have not done so already, share as much as you can with your sponsor about your spirituality and where you stand with it. Use the following exercise as a guideline.

Exercise 4-4: Sharing About Spirituality

Set a time for a meeting with your sponsor, or with someone you are considering asking to be your sponsor. Plan to meet for at least 45 minutes. The ideal location is one that will allow you to speak freely and without interruption.

Bring some or all of the notes that you have accumulated as you have moved through this book, along with any other information you have about your spirituality. Tell your sponsor that you would like to discuss and compare your spiritual paths to see how you can work with each other along these lines in recovery.

Focus on the words and phrases each of you uses when talking about spirituality and religion, and clear up any confusions as much as you can. And consider this exercise to be the first of many conversations on this subject.

Is it possible to work with a sponsor who has very different views from your own? The answer depends on whether you have mutual respect for each other and the ability to be open-minded about what others believe. I have seen atheists work well with church-goers, but only because neither was attempting to convince the other of what they must believe or think.

When you have a sponsor who knows how to focus on solutions rather than problems, and who is able to share his or her experience, strength, and hope, you will probably be able to work together no matter how different your beliefs. And if you have a sponsor who is trying to get you to change your spiritual ideas, consider whether they are pointing out a legitimate problem that you need to address. You may need to find someone else to sponsor you, but take a close look before you move on – a good sponsor sometimes asks difficult questions and it is not always comfortable to change, even when you need to.

Chapter Five

Being Vegetarian at the Potluck

"I was thrown out of college for cheating on the metaphysics exam: I looked into the soul of the boy next to me." — Woody Allen

Melinda walked into her first Twelve-Step meeting and began sorting people into categories – leaders, sheep, and rebels – just as she always had at other types of meetings. She spotted the leader, the person at the front of the room running the meeting; the sheep, sitting in chairs waiting to be called on; and a *lot* of rebels sprinkled among the flock.

"I sat in the back, so as not be noticed, and spent most of the meeting trying to figure out how it all worked, so I could fit in, if this is what I chose. My usual bravado was on the blink, and I didn't want to be noticed. I listened to people as they spoke, but couldn't really absorb what they were saying. My attention was scrambled and I was unable to adequately scan the room."

"After a few meetings, when my mind had cleared enough to really look around, I saw the Twelve Steps posted on the wall, and the word God within them in several places. My stomach tightened. Was this a religious group? Although I was desperately looking for a way to deal with my rotten life, I had eliminated the idea of God as an option years earlier, and I was not about to change my mind."

"However, I was desperate for a way to fix my miserable problems so I continued to attend meetings. After several more, a few people were greeting me by name, and I started to look forward to going. My defensiveness eased up enough for me to hear other people's ideas about the Twelve Steps, and I actually started to feel better about myself and life in general. Eventually, I was no longer the newest person in the room. And I began to believe people when they said I could define God any way I chose."

"Unfortunately, I reverted back to the God I was raised with. And this God was inconsistent, judgmental, granted favors based on worthiness, bestowed grace upon people who made donations or said particular prayers, and was basically an old man who required appeasement. I denied, both to myself and to everyone else, that I was still trying to win His favor. It took a few years and several shifts in my thinking before I could even begin to develop a new idea of spirituality."

"Occasionally, individual members of AA would get off track and give advice or opinions about what I should think or believe. But then someone else would remind them that 'the only requirement for membership is a desire to stop drinking,' and the person with the opinions would apologize. I had never experienced an entire group operating on such high principles."

"After many years in Twelve-Step recovery, I know that I am an equal member of the Program, and that nobody else can or should tell me what to believe about spirituality. It is like no other organization I have ever experienced."

Far from encouraging people to give up their individuality, the Twelve-Step programs are the only organizations I know of that have such unity among members without demanding that they think alike. All rebels are welcome!

How Meetings Work – Who's Running the Kitchen

When **Devon** was new to recovery, he was distrustful and uncomfortable about participating in a group: "Groups from my pre-recovery days typically had a 'pecking order' with the more outgoing members running the show, and the quieter members following along. While I still recognize that some personalities are stronger than others, nobody runs the Program. Some people take on various service positions, but they are there to serve, not to take charge."

"One of the first things I learned about meetings is that the person running the meeting is not a boss of any kind. Nobody in Twelve-Step recovery, including the people who appear to be in charge, can tell you what to think or what to do. You can learn how to be successful in your recovery by listening to other, more experienced members. But as you continue to listen, you will begin to notice that there are lots of ways to approach recovery and the Steps."

To better understand how recovery groups work without a leader, take a closer look at the Twelve Traditions. For example, part of Tradition Two of Alcoholics Anonymous states, "Our leaders are but trusted servants, they do not govern." This is a safeguard against big egos taking over, and if one should try, the group members know that by applying love and tolerance, as well as by pointing to the Traditions, eventually it will all smooth over.

Aggie learned about her own ego when she was elected to the position of steering committee head: "My job was to coordinate the monthly business meetings at which the group made its decisions. I was determined to raise the level of participation, and pushed people to attend. I also tried to initiate several changes. None of my attempts were successful, and I began to feel resentful and frustrated. A member with similar experience pulled me aside and quietly told me I had let my ego get in the way of my service to the group. I felt embarrassed, but it certainly cured the problem. After that, I stopped trying to control people and outcomes, and everything went much more smoothly."

Group Conscience – The True Democracy

How do all of these people manage to get along without rules? One especially useful Twelve-Step recovery tool is the "group conscience." Rather than having just a few people make decisions on behalf of the entire group, all group members discuss and vote on issues that relate to the group as a whole. When matters are discussed, the discussions go beyond simple majority rule. The members take time to listen to the minority opinion and to discuss it before taking a final vote. The result is usually that most, if not all, members are in agreement on any changes or decisions.

However, group conscience is more than just talking and voting. When a group conscience is taken, members are reminded to seek the presence and guidance of a loving Higher Power. To someone who is uncertain about God, or who is an atheist, this can mean focusing on our best and highest ideals, which are often called spiritual principles. Unselfishness, honesty, love, and the willingness to put the group ahead of individual whims are all principles that contribute to the best possible group decisions.

In the open and loving environment of a group conscience, everyone has an equal say in how the group operates. No matter how different, your opinions will be considered. Among other things, this ensures the meetings will remain unbiased about differences in spirituality. If, for example, someone in a meeting were trying to persuade others about a particular religion, you could bring it to the group for discussion. The group as a whole would then discuss how to resolve the situation.

Sometimes, individuals or even entire groups forget that they do not have the answers for everyone else. This is particularly true when it involves issues about God. The Traditions remind members that recovery is for everyone who wants it, and both the Steps and Traditions ensure that each of us can see God in our own way.

Fear of Brainwashing – Keeping Your Individuality in Recovery

There's a story going around about someone who told his sponsor he was afraid of being brainwashed, to which his sponsor replied, "If anyone ever needed to have his brain washed, it's you."

Nobody in Twelve-Step recovery wants you to become a mindless puppet, yet in meetings we remind ourselves that "the results were nil until we gave up absolutely." Is giving up the same as losing your individuality? Definitely not! Giving up does not mean imitating others or pretending to believe what you do not believe. It means getting real about what is in your heart and mind, being willing to honestly look at everything about yourself, accepting who you really are, and being willing to let go of the masks and the habits and behaviors that you hid behind. It can be difficult to recognize what's real from what is false, but if you are desperate for a new life, you will find the willingness to let go of any fear-based self-defensiveness that keeps you stuck.

Anna talks about how difficult letting go was for her: "I knew coming into recovery that I was willing to do whatever it took. But I had no idea how closed down I really was. I read the literature, went to lots of meetings, and got into service, starting with cleaning ashtrays and putting away chairs. Eventually I became a secretary and then, after a few years, I was elected to be a Group Service Representative. But I was kind of stiff about it all, kind of mechanical. I looked around a lot at what other people were doing, and constantly compared myself to them. I was about five years into the Program when I realized that I was wearing myself out trying to keep it all together and to get approval from everybody."

"I felt like I was being a good person, but something wasn't right. No matter what I did, I still felt like I needed to try to be perfect. I was always thinking about whether I was doing enough, or whether other people thought I was okay. But at some point, when I had been in the Program for about five years, something clicked inside of me, and I knew I couldn't live that way anymore."

"I realized no matter how hard I tried, I kept making mistakes anyway. I decided to let that be okay. Something had opened up inside, and it didn't matter so much how other people saw me. I was ready and willing to be exposed. Once I decided it was okay to be who I was and to accept my imperfections, I also stopped being so uncomfortable about being around other people."

"I feel free to share my ideas with the group now, and am not afraid to listen to other people talk about their ideas. I have opened up, the way you'd open the windows in a room that has been closed up for too long. The fresh air feels really good, and my mind didn't get 'polluted,' as I had feared."

Most people in recovery are initially concerned about being robbed of their individuality, but that concern usually begins to lift after a few meetings. If you are feeling pushed to conform by any meeting, go to a different meeting. When a group meets on a regular basis, it develops its own personality or flavor, and some will fit for you better than others. By trying out different meetings and by listening for similarities rather than being critical of the differences, you are likely to find at least one meeting that fits for you.

EXERCISE 5-1: PARTICIPATING IN A GROUP

Use the following steps to practice being part of a group without giving up your individuality.

1) Make a list of the benefits you are receiving by being part of a group, whether in or out of recovery. For example, group participation can elevate endorphins, the chemicals that provide us with a sense of well-being.

2) Recall a time in which you disagreed with a decision made by a group, then consider whether you continued to benefit from being part of that group, even after that disagreeable decision.

3) Attend a group meeting. While there, take a few minutes to consider your spiritual principles or Higher Power. As you do so, imagine the power of an entire room filled with people who are focusing on their own spiritual principles. This is the basis of a group conscience.

4) If you have unpleasant feelings as a result of this exercise, talk to some long-term members about how the group makes decisions and how they feel about that process.

Listening to Others – Take What You Like and Leave the Rest

I have heard people say in meetings that they made it in recovery when they stopped thinking so much and became willing to listen more to others. Not a bad idea, but how can you determine who to listen to and what to do when you get conflicting information? Here are some suggestions:

First, as soon as possible, get a sponsor. Find someone you identify with, someone who is an example of what you want to be as a recovering person. This person can then help you interpret what's going on and how things work in recovery, meetings, the Steps and Traditions, the literature, and often, many of the ways in which you interact with the world. Your sponsor is not responsible for helping you financially or for making your decisions or telling you what to do. But it's invaluable to have someone you trust who can give you the benefit of their experience.

Second, if the information or advice relates to the group, talk to some of the longer-term members of the group, or ask for a group conscience (see the first part of this chapter). For example, if you see someone or something disrupting a meeting, you do not need to take independent action to resolve the situation. Ask the group for help.

Lastly, learn to identify and trust your own inner wisdom. Each of us has the answers we need, but when first entering recovery, our ability to access our own intuition is often stunted as a result of self-destructive behavior. For a while, you may need a significant amount of input from your sponsor or a trusted friend. However, as you continue in recovery, your inner wisdom will gradually restore itself.

No matter how you translate the word God, the Serenity Prayer offers direction as we search for this highest part of ourselves: "God, grant me Serenity to accept the things I cannot change, Courage to change the things I can, and Wisdom to know the difference."

EXERCISE 5-2: ANTHROPOLOGICAL EXPEDITION

This exercise will give you practice listening to and interacting with others, without taking their opinions personally.

1) Arrange for a one-on-one meeting with someone you do not know well or who gets on your nerves a bit.

2) When you meet with them, spend as much time as possible listening without offering an opposing point of view. Just observe and learn about them, in much the same way an anthropologist would.

3) After your meeting, look at how this kind of objective, open listening changes the way you see the other person.

Staying Open – Keeping an Open Mind Without Losing the One You Have

The Twelve-Step model of recovery works for many people. It doesn't matter whether it is because God is working among us, or because we are simply supporting one another. Being willing to accept help is the key, and this willingness is a source of real power.

There is no way to compare AA or any other Twelve-Step program to existing organizations. The only focus of the Twelve-Step programs is recovery; not religion, not obedience, not conformity. Nobody can force you to participate. (If a Court of Law sentences someone to attend Twelve-Step meetings, the Twelve-Step community will not interfere, but it has absolutely no affiliation with the legal system or any other organization.)

One last note about being open to "spiritual experience," as **Mark** shares in his story: "For me, the spiritual experience was one of gradual internal resolution. Nobody ever pushed me into believing anything. I was cautious and took my time. Over a period of years, I have noticed a growing sense of connection with myself. This spirituality does not involve worshiping an external personality. I feel a comfort within myself, a sense that I am equipped with the ability to get the help I need when I need it; not necessarily from other people, but perhaps from nature or circumstance. I know it is more than just self-sufficiency. There is an open feeling about it, a lot like being a child in the safety of caring, responsible parents. Although my spirituality is not religious, it gives me a sense of the sacred. I enjoy the mystery of not being able to pin it down."

ϒϒϒ

> *"A mystery is that special kind of problem which for the human mind has no solution; the more we understand it, the more we become aware of additional factors relating to it that we do not understand. In mysteries what we know, and our realization of what we do not know, proceed together; the larger the island of knowledge, the longer the shoreline of wonder."* – from *The World's Religions* by Huston Smith

---

EXERCISE 5-3: A CLOSER LOOK AT OPEN-MINDEDNESS

One good way to identify open-mindedness or closed-mindedness is to observe others.

1) With as little judgment as possible, make a list of five people you know well, and whether you experience them as open- or closed-minded.

2) Note the behaviors and characteristics that go along with those labels. For example, note whether each of those people is fearful, generous of spirit, a good listener, a complainer, etc.

3) Review what you have written and look for patterns, especially where any of the traits apply to you.

You don't need to worry about losing your mind or your individuality in recovery. To the contrary, by participating in Twelve-Step recovery, you may begin to uncover who you really are.

Chapter Six

Meatless, Yet Hearty, Steps

*"A Zen master was asked by his students to explain the moon.
Without saying a word, he pointed his finger at the moon.
The students all gasped, looked at his hand, and said,
'Ah! The moon is a finger!' "*
–as related by Mel Ash in The Zen of Recovery

I cannot imagine how anyone who is desperate enough to go to a Twelve-Step recovery meeting could be completely comfortable with God or spirituality. It amazes me that anyone sticks around once they have read through the Twelve Steps. Perhaps the price of admission (hitting bottom, becoming completely miserable) is too great to give up on casually. Whatever your reason for looking at

Twelve-Step recovery, consider that most of the people who have checked it out were originally at odds with God or spirituality.

The ideas discussed in this chapter focus primarily on God in the Steps, and makes good use of the information you gathered in earlier chapters. However, this book barely scratches the surface when it comes to using the Steps in general. There are hundreds of excellent books and resources about using the Twelve Steps; please see the *Resources* section for more information about a few of them.

Note: The Twelve Steps below are from the original Twelve Steps of Alcoholics Anonymous (Copyright © A.A. World Services, Inc.). For other Twelve-Step programs, the language varies slightly.

Step One: We admitted we were powerless over alcohol – that our lives had become unmanageable.

The idea of powerlessness can seem ridiculous to people facing the insurmountable problems that drive them into Twelve-Step recovery. Without spirituality or inner resources, powerlessness would mean either a total collapse or an unbridled continuation of the original problematic behavior. Even without coming out and actually mentioning God or spirituality, the idea of spirituality is implied here, and it causes a lot of turmoil for people who are new to the Twelve Steps.

The Alcoholics Anonymous book, *Twelve Steps and Twelve Traditions*, says on page 21:

"We perceive that only through utter defeat are we able to take our first steps toward liberation and strength. Our admissions of personal powerlessness finally turn out to be firm bedrock upon which happy and purposeful lives may be built."

How can an admission of powerlessness be bedrock? By being willing to give up on the illusion of being in control, you become open to other sources of strength. Willpower is not enough, as you have probably come to understand through repeated failures at self-control. The source of strength that has allowed so many before you to succeed in Twelve-Step recovery is that indefinable power that some people call God. However, what is important to this discussion is that the word "God" serves only as a placeholder for your individual interpretation of the spiritual mystery.

Once again, I encourage you to put resistance aside for a time. Whether you think your inner power comes from God or not, consider the many millions of people who have honored some sense of sacredness, with or without a concept of God. The sacred is a combination of thought and feeling that fills us with awe as we walk through a springtime field of wildflowers or look into the eyes of a newborn child. You can explain it as simple human instinct, but nevertheless, it touches us in a way that is difficult to explain. And it is this type of experience and level of feeling from which I and many others draw inner strength and on which we base our own spirituality.

Admitting your inability to control your compulsive behavior is a necessary first step in successful recovery. Without this admission, you will be unable to entertain the openness toward spirituality or higher thought that is the core of successful recovery.

It may be that you are not able to let go of your attempts at self-control. You may fear, with good reason, that you will act out with wild abandon if you give yourself some slack. But by following in the footsteps of those who have gone before you, and by using the remaining Steps, you have a very good chance of developing the kind of spirituality or higher thought that will replace your desperate need to act compulsively. This is not about becoming a mindless follower. *It is about learning to access a higher level of thought in your own personal way.*

Step Two: Came to believe that a Power greater than ourselves could restore us to sanity.

The idea of admitting powerlessness in Step One could be a disaster if we were to stop there. Step Two carries us forward, beyond the state of personal powerlessness, into the next stage, which is to find a substitute for that power we thought we had. This is another point of great difficulty for many people. The obvious question is: how can you acknowledge a Power greater than yourself if you don't believe in or trust in God?

It is at this point that you most need to refer to the information you assembled as you read earlier chapters. This Power is what most people refer to as God, and you have been developing your own interpretation of what that means, based on your own individual spirituality.

The reference to restoring your sanity in this Step implies that you have been insane. This insanity is not necessarily limited to the insanity of your compulsive behavior, but refers also to what is behind your compulsive need to act out self-destructively. Why do *you* do these crazy things, when many others do not? Consider this definition of insanity, as taken from *Webster's New World Dictionary*. "Any form or degree of mental derangement or unsoundness of mind, permanent or temporary, that makes a person incapable of what is regarded legally as normal, rational conduct or judgment." If you reflect on the behavior that brings most of us to Twelve Step recovery programs, the definition fits uncomfortably well.

Put bluntly, there's probably something wrong with the way you think. Step Two suggests that you have a problem you cannot take care of without help. You have probably already figured that out, or you wouldn't be reading this. But how can you *acknowledge* a deity if you don't *believe* in one? How can you force your mind to change itself?

This time the answer lies in simple logic. You have been unable to control yourself. Others, with similar problems, have found a way to stop the behavior they previously could not control. *You need to find a way to follow their lead without letting them do the thinking for you.* This is where you need to draw from your own conclusions about spirituality and higher thought, in addition to being very clear about the powerlessness you admitted to in Step One.

It may even happen that this shift in thinking could restore you to a life free of the terrible compulsions that brought you to this point. You would not be the first person without a conventional idea of God to find comfort in the Twelve Steps.

Step Three: Made a decision to turn our will and our lives over to the care of God *as we understood Him.*

For those of us who bristle at references to the Judeo-Christian concept of God, this Step is particularly difficult. We are not people who can apply our existing faith to the task. We are faced, not only with the difficult circumstances of compulsions, but we also need to translate the language of the Steps.

This is the first time in the Twelve Steps that the word "God" is used outright, and it is tempered with the italicized phrase "as we understood Him." The men who wrote these Steps were not careless; they deliberately included a reminder about the importance of being true to our *individual* understanding of God.

This obstacle has been overcome by many before you. The advice that helped me most was simply "Don't be so literal."

Semantics – the way words are understood and misunderstood – provides a full-time career for some people. It is especially difficult to be precise or to adequately convey meaning when describing ideas such as spirituality and higher thought.

Most of the people I know who have long-term success in Twelve-Step recovery are quick to admit that they cannot define God, no matter what their beliefs. The concept is unexplainable, resulting in such names as "Divine Mystery" and "Unknowable Source." And many of those same long-term members say that, had they not experienced the insanity of their compulsive behavior, they would not have been forced to search for that spirituality. They are grateful!

ΎΎΎ

> *"Every man and woman who has joined A.A. and intends to stick has, without realizing it, made a beginning on Step Three. Isn't it true that, in all matters touching upon alcohol, each of them has decided to turn his or her life over to the care, protection, and guidance of A.A.? Already a willingness has been achieved to cast out one's own will and one's own ideas about the alcohol problem in favor of those suggested by A.A. Now if this is not turning one's will and life over to a new-found 'Providence,' then what is it?"*
> – from *Twelve Steps and Twelve Traditions,* p35

It doesn't seem to matter whether you begin with atheism, a Judeo-Christian God, or another, highly individualized way of approaching spirituality. The important thing is to be open to the experience, and to walk through the Steps in order to find your way to what is true for you.

Letting go always makes me think of the Indiana Jones movie in which Harrison Ford's character hesitantly follows instructions to step forward even without anything solid to step onto. He steps forward into what looks like a bottomless gorge, only to discover that there was a step beneath him all along, one that he could not see. The authors of the Twelve Steps undoubtedly knew what they were asking of us — to have faith in something undefined, and to trust that we will come out okay by putting ourselves in a new frame of mind.

Step Four: Made a searching and fearless moral inventory of ourselves.

Being sensitive to the God thing, **Judy** was immediately suspicious of the word "moral" in this Step: "This word had been used as a club by some religious people in my life, representatives for a judgmental God who dictated what was moral and what was not. While I saw the usefulness of getting real with myself, I resented the idea of 'right vs. wrong.'"

"However, an intense desire to feel better kept me moving ahead, listening to what my sponsor had to say, reading about this Step (and all the Steps), and letting go of my resistance. Just as with the earlier Steps, I had to do some translating. As I frequently do, I looked to the dictionary, and to my surprise, religion was not mentioned anywhere in the definitions for 'moral.' It was about ethical behavior, which I believe contributes to the greater good."

When you evaluate your own behavior, in doing the Fourth Step or elsewhere, try replacing the terms "good and bad" with "what works and what doesn't work." Punching someone in the nose is not an offense against God, but it is an act that has consequences that may be unfavorable. The act itself is not necessarily bad if you consider the motivation. It determines whether you feel regret, self-recrimination, or shame, or whether you feel that you acted in the best possible way in the service of others as well as yourself.

The Fourth Step can help you see a bigger picture of yourself and to recognize the habits and behaviors that make you unhappy. By identifying which parts of your internal house need cleaning, remodeling, or repair, you might not need to escape into self-destructive behavior so often, and the remaining Steps will continue to carry you forward.

Fourth Step Inventory

Many suggested formats for the Step Four inventory exist. Here's one that works well for every type of spirituality.

1) In looking back over your life, which memories are still painful? Are still guilt-ridden? Are still dirty?
2) In what ways today do you feel inadequate as a person?
3) Who do you resent, and why? Be as specific (and as nasty!) as possible.
4) What do you consider to be your defects of character as you see them?
5) What do you conceive to be the ongoing problems in your human relationships, the issues that provoke the same reactions time after time?
6) What do you consider to be your defects of character as you see them?
7) What, today, are your goals in life, whether realistic or not?
8) How do you think that Twelve-Step recovery can, in any way, start you toward any of these goals?

— With gratitude to Clancy I.

Step Five: Admitted to God, to ourselves, and to another human being the exact nature of our wrongs.

It was a challenge for **Adriana** to face her Fourth-Step list, and she was extremely uncomfortable about reading it to her sponsor: "Admitting it to God seemed impossible, since my idea of God didn't involve a being that could hear me. I got through this by imagining each secret I harbored as a piece of broken glass that I had swallowed. This Step was my chance to cough it all up so it would stop cutting up my insides. I wasn't necessarily confessing to some higher being, but was releasing all of it from within myself."

"One surprising result occurred in the process of doing this Step. After seeing my inventory in black and white, and then reading it to my sponsor, I had to admit that the judge of whom I was most afraid was actually myself. It was my own self-condemnation I had been avoiding, rather than that of the God I had discarded."

The process of the Fifth Step can be immensely freeing if you are willing to take an honest look at how you judge yourself. It's one thing to understand the concept intellectually, but having the courage to put your inventory out in the open is a true indication of how you feel about yourself and how you feel about the opinions of others. Apply your own idea of God to this Step, or ignore the God idea altogether and do the Step anyway. As with the previous Steps, it will help relieve the compulsion that created chaos in your life.

Step Six: Were entirely ready to have God remove all these defects of character.

The first time **Margo** approached this Step, her intention was to become perfect: "Armed with the knowledge of what I needed to change about myself, I was all set to fix myself and all my problems. Or so I thought. I embarked on a series of attempts to become virtuous and above reproach. I am happy to say none of these worked."

"I had not realized that my behavior is not controllable by my willpower. I was able to admit, in the First Step, that I could not control my drinking. But I still thought I could control everything else about myself. It astonished me to watch myself repeating behavior I had vowed to stop."

"This Step has become one of my most valued tools, in recovery and in life. I have learned that willpower is not the way to become a better person. It is the act of appealing to a Higher Power – in my case, the higher part of myself – that has helped me change over time."

If you want to learn how to be comfortable in your own skin, take a close look at the Sixth Step. Replace the word "God" with whatever you perceive that power to be. Then be willing to give this new way of "self-improvement" a try.

Step Seven: Humbly asked Him to remove our shortcomings.

In Step Six, you are asked to be willing to replace willpower with an appeal to your higher nature or your own spirituality. Step Seven suggests that you ask to have your shortcomings *removed*. My husband, who was a counselor in a Twelve-Step-based recovery program for many years, explains it this way, "Step Six asks us to put our shortcomings into a cosmic garbage can, and Step Seven asks us to put the can on the curb for pickup." The sticking place for many of us is about who or what picks up the can!

You are the only one who can decide this. The most important thing to remember is that you are not going to be hauling the garbage can off to the dump on your own. This Step is primarily about humility. You are not capable of using your own mind to fix the difficulties you have within your own mind.

One of the best books I have encountered on the Twelve Steps is *A Skeptics Guide to the Twelve Steps* by Phillip Z. (see *Resources* for additional information). In it, he explains "A theme that recurs throughout program literature is that we can take action and apply great effort to the tasks of recovery, but deep psychic changes come about outside our conscious control. In order to work Step Seven, I must bring my will to the task of acting in new ways, while at the same time recognizing that whatever psychic changes occur are up to my Higher Power."

You do not need to have God in your life in order to have a Higher Power. Put your ego aside, look to whatever it is that causes you to desire love, goodness, and growth, and then get out of the way. If you are resistant to prayer, I urge you to do your best with it for now. The Seventh Step Prayer may require a lot of translation (from the Judeo-Christian language to your own), but it beautifully conveys the attitude of humility that Step Seven asks of us:

"My Creator, I am now willing that you should have all of me, good and bad. I pray that you now remove from me every single defect of character which stands in the way of my usefulness to you and my fellows. Grant me strength, as I go out from here, to do your bidding. Amen."

This prayer mentions "good and bad" but just as in the Fourth Step, I suggest replacing these judgmental words with the idea of "what works and what doesn't work" in your life, based on how well your life is working, and on your own values and spirituality.

Step Eight: Made a list of all persons we had harmed, and became willing to make amends to them all.

For some, this Step makes recovery seem impossibly difficult. For **Andrew**, it was a relief, because it appeared to be one of the few Steps that didn't involve God: "I started to make a list, and looked ahead a bit to imagine myself apologizing to some people.

Yet, as I talked with my sponsor and read some Program literature, this Eighth Step involved some subtleties I hadn't considered."

"The spiritual groundwork I had done proved invaluable as I continued with my list. A list of what I had *done* was not enough. As directed, I also looked for the ways in which my *attitudes* – the ideas I had about life and my place in it – had affected others."

Review your relationships with people and organizations by looking through the eyes of your own values. If you believe kindness is important, how do you feel about the way you pushed your younger brother away for so many years? If you believe in honesty, what about the lies you told your last employer about being sick on so many Monday mornings?

Admitting the not-so-obvious harm you caused may be what frees you most.

Step Nine: Made direct amends to such people wherever possible, except when to do so would injure them or others.

This is the apology and restitution Step. The first time **Richie** read it, he wasn't particularly worried, because he had never stolen large sums of money or committed serious crimes: "Frankly, I felt smug. My list was short, and focused mostly on my ex-wife and my son, whom I had essentially abandoned for drinking and related behaviors. Once again, I was relieved to see that there was no mention of God. But it was during this Step that I really began to see I am living in a world that goes beyond my ability to explain and comprehend."

"After working the earlier Steps, I had begun to let go of my resistance and my thinking had cleared up a bit. I was still opposed to the idea of an external God with a personality. But something I could not explain was happening. Coincidences were occurring at such a rate that I began to doubt they were purely coincidental."

"One of the most amazing occurrences was that people, as I added them to my list and made up my mind to make amends to them, would suddenly reappear in my life. A former friend, whom I had not yet looked up, appeared beside me on a street corner in a town neither of us had ever visited. We walked to a nearby bakery, where the words came out of me without effort."

"In a similar way, many of the other people on my list turned up, and the Ninth Step seemed to work itself. Doing the Ninth Step changed me in ways I would never have suspected. I now understand why the Promises are given at this stage of recovery."

It's fairly obvious that making amends would make you feel better about yourself. But there is more afoot than straightforward psychological shifts. If you put your best effort towards working the Steps with an open mind, by the time you get to Step Nine, you can expect both internal and external changes to occur.

No matter what you believe, these changes will indicate the existence of a power greater than you alone can muster. Call it whatever you like – this power is available to us all.

ϒϒϒ

> *"I admit that I need more strength than I alone possess to overcome the compulsion to drink. I receive this strength from the power for good generated in A.A. I have interpreted the frequent mention of 'God' in the Twelve Steps and elsewhere as power that comes from other people."* – from the AA pamphlet: *Do You Think You're Different – Ed's Story*

Step Ten: Continued to take personal inventory, and when we wrong, promptly admitted it.

Rosetta started this Step by monitoring every thought, every action, every mood, and nearly paralyzed herself as she tried to do it all perfectly: "I laugh about it now, and refer to myself back then as a 'psychochondriac.' I mistook 'paying attention and taking responsibility for my actions' to mean 'being hypervigilant in order to prevent myself from making any mistakes.' It's actually a lot easier than I made it. As I understand it now, Step Ten means to be a non-judgmental witness to yourself."

Observe what works and what doesn't, make amends if you do something to cause a problem or a hurt, and learn as you go. This Step means no mistakes are wasted because they help us find, through trial and error, more effective ways to think and behave.

If you tend to be self-critical, resolve to lighten up as you do this Step. Simply notice what you're doing, looking for selfishness, dishonesty, resentment, or fear. Observe without harsh criticism, just as you would if you were watching a beloved child who is learning to walk and is stumbling along the way. Notice your missteps, then try a different maneuver the next time you encounter a similar situation. Remind yourself that if there is no traditional version of God judging you, then it is only you who fills out your report card. You are free to be yourself.

If you are one who tends to blame others for everything, watch yourself with an eye towards recognizing how you affect the world around you. If you approach someone with a scowl, don't be surprised when they treat you badly. If you feel a sense of entitlement, you are interrupting the flow of those fabulous coincidences that happen to people who are enjoying what they already have. In any situation that pulls you into resentment or judgment, ask yourself how you contributed to what happened, and be as honest as possible with the answer.

The Tenth Step will help you spot mistakes sooner rather than later, which in turn makes your internal life run more smoothly. For many of us, it smoothes our external lives as well.

Step Eleven: Sought through prayer and meditation to improve our conscious contact with God as we understood Him, praying only for the knowledge of His will for us and the power to carry that out.

Step Eleven raised so much resistance in **Kevin** that he experienced a crisis: "I had developed a personal code that defined my spirituality, but which did not require that I pray or meditate. I believed meditation was a gimmick, and that I could certainly control my own mind without burning incense. But I also recognized that I felt emptier than I ever had, now that drinking and compulsive behavior were not filling the void."

"Determined to find some deeper meaning in my life, I began to explore different ideas about spirituality. I visited several churches and eventually latched onto a new thought church. They talked about the power of the mind as the source of spiritual power, and instead of prayer, they used 'treatments.' It worked for me, and as I look back, I see that the biggest difference between that church and more traditional Christian churches was the language. Many of the same elements were there, but the judgmental God was nowhere to be found."

"The experience helped me open my mind to new possibilities and even provided insight into the usefulness of meditation. I learned many different ways to meditate – with quiet music or guiding words playing into my headphones, by taking a walk on the beach, by chanting a phrase that is sacred to me, by simply sitting and allowing myself to do nothing at all – and I continue to find new ways all the time."

"For me now, praying is about focusing on a specific idea and turning it over to the The Universe (my phrase for God). Meditation is about letting my mind and heart revitalize themselves. It is not something my brain can figure out."

If you are absolutely convinced that there is no mystery beyond logic or nothing your brain cannot grasp, have the courage to go exploring. Listen to other people in recovery as they talk about Step Eleven. Explore other forms of spirituality to see if anything in particular fits. Try some of the more scientific approaches to meditation, such as tones that calm brain activity, or deep breathing that slows the heart rate.

ϒϒϒ

> *"When the alcoholic turns to God, he meets an old adversary. The prayers of the alcoholic, long uttered in the despair of loneliness, are unanswered – at least in a form he is prepared to accept. The resentments he has about God, and most alcoholics have many, make it very difficult for him to encounter God, even if he were free of the alcoholic haze. Whatever notions he has about God from his childhood, from his upbringing, from his adolescence, they all need to be relinquished, because – like everything else about the alcoholic – they have become part of his disease."*
> – from *Steps of Transformation*, by Father Meletios Webber

Whatever you do, don't miss out on the benefits of this Step. It can create a sense of serenity that is also powerful. By calming your mind, your instincts are sharpened and your thinking is clearer. This Step is not only spiritual, it is also practical.

Step Twelve: Having had a spiritual awakening as the result of these steps, we tried to carry this message to alcoholics and to practice these principles in all our affairs.

After working the earlier Steps, most people feel mentally, emotionally, and spiritually changed. Some feel reborn, but the spiritual change is usually less dramatic for those of us who invent or re-invent our spirituality. Nevertheless, a sense of deeper meaning or purpose usually occurs.

Although dwelling on the past is not normally a good idea, reaching Step Twelve is a good time to look back at your earliest days in recovery and compare what you were like then to what you are like now. You probably feel better about yourself and your interactions with other people. You are likely to have an appreciation for the Twelve Steps and for recovery in general. Spiritual growth and spiritual awakening are subjective terms, but if you can cast aside your prejudices against the word "spiritual," you will identify at least some new awareness. You will then be able to share your new attitudes and ideas with people who might be feeling hopeless.

The Twelfth Step is the time at which you can make a deliberate effort to be of service in recovery if you have not already done so. You can remember what you were like in the beginning, and when new people arrive, you can welcome them and share the ways in which you approached recovery and how you changed as a result. You can take on a service position, such as group treasurer or representative, depending on how much time in recovery is suggested for these jobs. There are many ways to be of service.

Eileen talks about how she believes service is actually selfish, because it makes her feel great: "I no longer need to hear appreciation, although I still enjoy hearing it. I am fully aware that what I do will benefit me as much if not more than it benefits others. I am a sponsor to other people now, and this lets me learn from their mistakes without always having to make my own. I also get to see how sharing my mistakes can sometimes help others to avoid the same errors or to be easier on themselves when they do make mistakes, and this feels good."

"I have learned to apply this Step to my entire life, rather than just using it in recovery. I am more patient with people, both strangers and those I know well. My road rage has disappeared. I have good friends with whom I share mutual respect. I am able to be honest with myself and others, and my relationships with my family have improved beyond my wildest hopes."

"Best of all, I love and like myself, and the self-respect seems to engender respect and love from others. I no longer crumble when I find the inevitable few who don't like me. I spend less energy trying to get approval, and have more to spare when it comes to being of service. I take good care of myself and my belongings, yet my finances and my material possessions no longer define who I am."

By the time you get to Step Twelve, you might not even need to be reading this. But if you *have* done this Step and are still not feeling that "spiritual awakening," do not give up. Just as you are encouraged to take one day at a time, you are also encouraged not to give up just before the miracle happens.

No matter what you believe, these Steps can make a profound difference in your life. Keep an open mind, and if you do decide that the Twelve Steps aren't doing it for you, explore the *Resources* section for a list of alternatives. Don't give up – life is too good to miss.

Chapter Seven

Cold Leftovers and Suggestions for Reheating

*"What we really have is a daily reprieve contingent
on the maintenance of our spiritual condition."*
– *Alcoholics Anonymous*

At some point in recovery, if you stick around long enough, part or all of your Twelve-Step program may begin to feel stale. This often occurs when the "pink cloud" of early recovery wears thin. Most of the people who reported their experience with this had been in recovery for two to seven years.

Even more difficult are those times when, after experiencing varying degrees of internal comfort over several years of recovery, your spirituality seems to dissolve. Where there was once a sense of well-being, an uncomfortable grayness or even a sense of despair or loss of connection sets in.

This chapter offers ideas for breathing new life into a fading spirituality, regaining your spiritual foothold when you have lost it, and expanding and deepening the spirituality you have now.

The First Spiritual Crisis in Recovery – How to Survive

Whether or not you call it a "pink cloud," there is often a sense of relief and even euphoria once you have immersed yourself in the Program. Your original addiction or compulsion releases its hold, the major problems you started with begin to clear up, and life feels better than it has in a long time.

Eventually, however, that internal sense of relief lessens, either suddenly or gradually. Restlessness, boredom, and irritability begin to intrude. Praying and meditating, no matter how well they had been working for you, lose their effectiveness, and you feel resistant and unwilling to go through the motions. Whether you are an atheist, a fervent believer in a particular creed, or somewhere in between, you feel lost and uncertain about your personal spirituality.

Narcotics Anonymous addresses this very well:

> "Even after years clean, when we have been working a program of recovery and seeking change, we may at times experience periods when life seems meaningless. We may experience a sense of alienation too painful to ignore.

At such times, we may find ourselves moving away from sanity, not toward it. We may begin to question our commitment to recovery. We can become obsessed with self-destructive thoughts. We may feel an urge to fall back on what seems easier: the familiar ways of our addiction. During these times, we need to renew our commitment to recovery. We trust that we are undergoing a fundamental transformation, even though we may not yet understand its full implication for our lives. As painful as it seems, we must change. If we trust that there is growth despite the pain, we can walk through these difficult periods more readily." – ©, Narcotics Anonymous World Services Inc., Van Nuys, CA, *It Works: How and Why*, p. 25. Reprinted by permission. All rights reserved.

As you seek to regain comfort, you review all the tools and resources you have learned about, but no obvious solution comes to mind. This is the time to reach for help from others.

Start by talking with your sponsor. None of us can see ourselves as objectively as a trusted advisor can, and your sponsor may have some valuable information. Just as a doctor would check your vital signs and basic functions if you were ill, your sponsor can help you run a check on the basic health of your recovery program.

Are you sure you are getting to as many meetings as you need? Maybe it's time to get back to doing Step work, if you have stopped. Take a look at your attitudes. Have you been judgmental or bored in meetings? Have you been of service lately? If you are sponsoring others, are you sponsoring too few or too many, or letting your ego get too wrapped up in the results?

Once you have taken an honest look at how you have been functioning in recovery, be willing to take action. Focus on the solution rather than on the problem to get yourself back on track. Let the safety of the group carry you along until this feeling passes. It *will* pass – as you reach the next level of growth.

ϓϓϓ

> *"They think it necessary to the existence of divine truth, that he who once had possession of it should never finally lose it."*   – William Cowper

---

EXERCISE 7-1: ACT AS IF

One approach that may be helpful is to repeat some of what you did as a newcomer. Do one or more of the following:

1) Start over with the Twelve Steps, reading the literature available in your Program, and talk about your readings with your sponsor.

2) Volunteer to do the least glamorous service position in your group, such as cleanup or setting up chairs, for at least the next few weeks. Be sure you do this for your own gratification, rather than for praise or approval.

3) Reach out to some newcomers, being sure to talk little and listen much.

4) At every meeting for at least the next several weeks, say hello to at least two people you don't know or don't normally talk with.

5) Take a few minutes to think back to the feelings of relief and gratitude you felt in early recovery.

These are not "instant cures." Just as early recovery took some time to take hold, these spiritual slumps can also take time to move through.

I Should Be Better – Fading Spirituality in Long-Term Recovery

Suzanne was just beginning to think she was catching on to a sane and comfortable way of living, after being in Twelve-Step programs for several years, when she fell apart again: "For no reason in particular, for weeks I cried at every meeting, and I was tired of listening to myself. I thought I was supposed to be an example of what people would want to be like in sobriety, but why would anyone want what I have if I didn't even want it myself?"

"I incorrectly believed that, by using the tools of the Program, I would be spared from the difficulties of life."

"Now that I have been through several of these 'gray zones,' whether they are induced by outer events or inner growth spurts, I am less discouraged. During these times, however, I still feel the pain and the desperate desire to get back to a more comfortable mental and emotional state. It feels tremendously embarrassing to be so off balance. I whine and cry and search for a way out, and each time, my head tells me even though I have always gotten through these difficult times in the past, this time could be different — I could be stuck in this place forever!"

"I have learned the hard way to stay in practice with the tools of the Program. By maintaining close relationships with other members and my sponsor, being of service, using the Steps, reading literature, and going to meetings, it is a lot easier to get out of a ditch when I do fall into one."

Jim McGregor describes the ebb and flow of life beautifully on page 33 in *The Tao of Recovery*:

Returning

Like the tides, the clouds, the sun, and the flow of the universe itself, I move away and back again.

Sometimes it is frightening to lose my sense of well-being. Always it is unpleasant.

In the natural order there are excesses and scarcities such as floods and droughts, violent storms and doldrums. But things return to normal.

Why would I expect to be above the natural order? The awareness that I am a part of the natural order is an indescribable gift.

I am grateful.

If you want to minimize your stays in the gray zones or otherwise painful times, maintaining a spiritual condition is especially important. Yet, of course, it's difficult to maintain the same enthusiasm that many of us had in early recovery. As Bill W. says in Chapter 7 of *Alcoholics Anonymous*, "It is easy to let up on the spiritual program of action and rest on our laurels. We are headed for trouble if we do, for alcohol is a subtle foe. We are not cured of alcoholism. What we really have is a daily reprieve contingent on the maintenance of our spiritual condition." These words are just as true for any type of Twelve-Step program.

Once you have designed your own spirituality, it is not enough to recognize it and then to set it on a shelf. Even if you actively work towards spiritual growth, there are times when you could benefit by refreshing or revising your spiritual practice.

EXERCISE 7-2: REFRESHING YOUR SPIRITUAL PRACTICE

To move from the gray zone back into the rainbow of spirituality, do one or both of the following:

1) Take an honest look at what you are doing on a regular basis to maintain your spirituality and replace anything that is "stale." For example, if you have listened to the same guided meditation for a while and find yourself drifting off, seek out a new guided meditation or even a completely new way of meditating.

2) Go on a spiritual outing. This could be walking along the ocean, taking a weekend retreat, hiking through your favorite regional park, or planting flowers in the garden. Just be sure you break away from the ordinary to refresh your inner connection.

Dark Night of the Soul – Spiritual Pain

Throughout time, many of the world's most spiritual and religious figures have undergone a period of painful disconnection from spirituality. Not merely a gray zone, it has been described as utter darkness. St. John of the Cross described it as the "dark night of the soul," and said:

> "(it) puts the sensory spiritual appetites to sleep, deadens them, and deprives them of the ability to find pleasure in anything. It binds the imagination, and impedes it from doing any good discursive work. It makes the memory cease, the intellect become dark and unable to understand anything, and hence it causes the will to become arid and constrained, and all the faculties empty and useless. And over this hangs a dense and burdensome cloud, which afflicts the soul, and keeps it withdrawn from the good."

It is a period of suffering that can occur to anyone on a spiritual search, one that includes profound loneliness, the complete absence of light and hope, and a feeling of being able to go neither forward nor back. Struggling does not help, and may even make you feel worse.

Carol talks of just such a difficult time in her life: "During that agonizing time, I felt as though all the parts of me had been put in a jar and shaken violently. I felt at a loss for words, and joked later that I had 'lost my lines.' The consolation of friends was meaningless. I felt misunderstood, not only by others but by myself, as well. Nobody could fix me."

"I went through the motions of each day, wondering what life really meant to me, if anything. The world seemed unfair and cruel. And I could not think of a single thing I would truly enjoy. I tried writing, praying, talking to my sponsor, meeting with a counselor, sleeping more, exercising more. I even considered suicide, but I wasn't entirely sure it would result in peace, and there was always the chance that I would botch it."

If you are experiencing this kind of pain, there is one thing to remember above all else. *Do not return to your self-destructive behavior.* Trust the process as best you can. Know that you are not the first one to go through this. Be gentle with yourself, just as you would if you were going through a major illness or surgery. Eat well, do one thing at a time, keep going to meetings, get plenty of sleep, and don't try to force a remedy. One very important recommendation: Avoid the temptation to make drastic changes in your outer world, such as moving to another city, changing your job, or getting a divorce. This is a time of internal revisions, a battle between your innermost self and your ego. External changes are not likely to help, and may even prolong your pain.

Spiritual pain can be another way of "hitting bottom," similar to the way many feel just before reaching out for recovery. And you can move through it.

Bob describes the experience of coming out the other end:

"Completely defeated, and with nothing to hang on to, I eventually surrendered to the pain. And then, as though I had walked outside after a spring rain, I felt cleaned out. And along with that feeling was a real sense of freedom and lightness."

Times of profound change or confusion require adjustment, including spiritual adjustment. No matter how sure you have been about God or spirituality, your mind and heart constantly take in new information, and often, this incoming information reaches a critical mass. Like a catch-all closet, you can only cram so much in before there isn't any more room. Letting go, reorganizing, taking inventory, and being scrupulous about what to keep and what to let go of are all part of putting life back in order again.

EXERCISE 7-3: ACTIVE SURRENDERING

This exercise includes several approaches to letting go of spiritual pain. Do one or more of the following:

1) If you have an altar or a special area dedicated to prayer or meditation, take it completely apart. Remove every significant item. Instead of praying or meditating in that space, just sit quietly for ten-to-twenty minutes at a time, doing absolutely nothing. Recreate the area at a later time, when you feel better.

2) Make a date with your sponsor or a trusted friend and ask for some time to talk about your pain, frustration, and resistance. No apologies, evaluations, or remedies should be part of the conversation. This is just a cleansing, and nothing new should be added to your spiritual mind. Keep it clear and open so that your Higher Self can later replace what was lost.

3) Select the medium that allows you to be your most expressive — drawing, skiing, writing, dancing, singing, wood carving, sewing, or whatever else sets you free. Use it to express your frustration, rather than trying to create something of value. For example, if you paint or write, smear the paper with black, or gouge holes into it. Let the darkness express itself so it can move on.

4) Go on a retreat or find a place at which you can be completely at ease. Spend a few days just being yourself, with no obligations. Remind yourself frequently during this time that your spirituality will find you, rather than you needing to search for it. Expect nothing.

5) Take as much time as possible to do something absolutely mindless, yet does not fill your mind (no television). Start a 3,000-piece jigsaw puzzle, pull weeds, doodle, or paint a wall. Just be in the moment. If you find yourself trying to resolve problems or make plans, simply notice and return your mind to the project at hand.

Above all else, let the process unfold at its own pace. It is often the case that deep spiritual shifts take time and cause considerable discomfort. As you move through this time, remain as involved in the Program as you would if you were a newcomer – because you are.

Refreshers – Keeping Spirituality Interesting

No matter how effective or worthwhile any activity has ever been for me, I have at some point become restless or bored with it. Sometimes all it takes to restore interest is a small change. At other times, I have made major changes, such as finding a new career or beginning a whole new exercise program.

Carl describes this need for change and how he applies it to his recovery: "Whether it's a favorite meditation tape, a particular prayer routine, or the meetings I attend, I can't seem to keep going through the same motions endlessly, over and over. In my distant past, I would force myself to work through the drudgery until I could not continue, and all activity would cease. I have abandoned exercise for years at a time, changed jobs, hobbies, friends, and even wives when I lost interest. I was worried, then, when I started to lose interest in the habits I had developed as part of my Twelve-Step recovery program."

"Others have shared similar experience with me, and from them, I learned not to 'throw the baby out with the bathwater.'

When I get tired of meditation, I find another way to meditate. I take service positions and keep my commitments, but when the time is up, I move on to something new. And I keep my eyes open for new approaches to spirituality."

Don't let any of your spiritual practices wear out their welcome. While there are times when you may need to push yourself a bit into taking needed action, it is also reasonable to have as much fun as possible. Be creative with recovery and spirituality. In the same way a bicyclist can buy a new helmet or an artist can switch from acrylics to watercolors, you can make changes that will keep your spiritual program alive and stimulating.

Here are some ideas for keeping your spirituality fresh:

- Do at least one nice thing every day for someone without getting caught. If you get caught or if you tell anyone, it doesn't count.

- Try a new way of meditating, such as buying a new guided meditation CD or joining a meditation group. Learn to do a walking meditation. There are hundreds of books and recordings about meditation that can offer new approaches.

- Go "back to basics" by doing the Twelve Steps again, from the beginning

- Go to 90 meetings in 90 days.

- Do a Tenth Step in writing at the end of each day for at least two weeks.
- Check the Internet for "spiritual films," and watch a few.
- Borrow someone else's Higher Power for a few weeks.
- Write your own prayer and use it for a while on a daily basis.
- If you are lucky enough to have a newborn child around, sit and look into his or her eyes.
- Go on a silent retreat.
- Shop for sacred music. Really listen to it.

Or, make up your own refreshers. The recommendations provided in each Twelve-Step recovery program are not supposed to be miserable or boring. "We are not a glum lot." It's up to you to be happy. By keeping recovery fresh and new, you will help yourself, and you will be an example to others of what true success in recovery is all about: being happy, joyous, and free.

A Final Word – Going Out From Here

Many people have experienced the *desperation* that is called "hitting bottom," the *hesitation* and *cynicism* of new recovery, the *elation* of new-found spirituality, and the *ups and downs* of life in ongoing recovery. And many of those same people still have a "daily reprieve" from self-destructive behavior and addiction. Being willing to let go of defensiveness and being open to accept help and to consider new ideas have been key ingredients in their recipes for success.

Where independence was once praised as the psychological ideal, interdependence is now recognized as a true component of mental health. But it takes courage to give and take, to be emotionally honest, and to be vulnerable with others in relationship. For those in recovery, it takes even more courage to experience relationships without the crutch of addictive behavior.

What gives so many the willingness and the courage to accept help from others? At first, it's desperation that pushes many into recovery. And then, it's the joy of being fully alive and happy that keeps them there. Many people in successful, ongoing recovery know a joy and happiness that exceeds their greatest expectations. Spirituality – no matter how you choose to define it – is at the core of this happiness.

Life still happens, of course. People die, difficulties arise, relationships and things and circumstances change whether we want them to or not. But with a spiritual foundation, one that grows as we move through each day's experiences, there is nothing we cannot handle. Nurture your spirituality, the way that works best for you, and enjoy your life, *one day at a time.*

RESOURCES

This section lists just a few of the many programs, books, and websites that you can use to obtain additional information about the topics covered in this book.

Programs for Recovery

TWELVE-STEP RECOVERY PROGRAMS

The alphabetized list below includes some, but not all, of the programs that integrate some form of the Twelve Steps for various types of recovery.

- Adult Children Of Alcoholics
- Al-Anon/Alateen
- Alcoholics Anonymous
- Co-Dependents Anonymous
- Cocaine Anonymous
- Debtors Anonymous
- Dual Recovery Anonymous
- Emotions Anonymous
- Gamblers Anonymous
- Incest Survivors Anonymous
- Marijuana Anonymous
- Naranon
- Narcotics Anonymous
- Overeaters Anonymous
- Rape Survivors Anonymous

- Recoveries Anonymous
- Recovering Couples Anonymous
- Sex and Love Addicts Anonymous
- Sexaholics Anonymous
- Sexual Compulsives Anonymous
- Survivors of Incest Anonymous
- Workaholics Anonymous

For contact information about these Anonymous programs, check your local telephone directory, or see *Websites of Interest*, below, for Internet links.

ALTERNATIVE RECOVERY PROGRAMS

LifeRing Secular Recovery
A non-religious, self-help recovery organization for individuals who seek group support to achieve abstinence from alcohol and other addictive drugs.
LifeRing Service Center, 1440 Broadway, Suite 312, Oakland, CA 94612-2023. Tel: 510 763 0779. www.lifering.org

Women for Sobriety
Self-help program for women who wish to overcome alcoholism and other addictions. Non-12-step; has a female-empowerment perspective.
Women For Sobriety, Inc., PO Box 618, Quakertown, PA 18951-0618. Tel: (215) 536-8026. www.womenforsobriety.org

SMART Recovery

Self-Management and Recovery Training. Non-religious recovery program, guided by principles of rational-emotive behavior therapy. SMART Recovery, 7537 Mentor Ave., Suite 306, Mentor, OH 44060. Tel: Toll free: 866-951-5357. www.smartrecovery.org/

Rational Recovery Center

Non-religious, for-profit recovery program offering alternatives to the methods of AA.

Rational Recovery Center, Box 800, Lotus, CA 95651

Tel: 530-621-4374. www.rational.org

Books

TWELVE-STEP PROGRAM LITERATURE

Each Twelve-Step program has at least a few "official" books. They are too numerous to list here. Instead, this is an abbreviated list of major titles that have been quoted from in this book. For other Twelve-Step books, see the websites for individual programs (later in this appendix), or check your local library or recovery bookstore.

———, *Alcoholics Anonymous.* New York: Alcoholics Anonymous World Services, Inc., 1939, 1955, 1976, 2001.

———, *Came To Believe*. New York: Alcoholics Anonymous World Services, Inc., 1973.

———, *How It Works And Why*. Van Nuys: Narcotics Anonymous World Service Office, Inc., 1993.

———, *Twelve Steps and Twelve Traditions*. New York: Alcoholics Anonymous World Services, Inc., 1952, 1953, 1981, 1993.

OTHER TWELVE STEP BOOKS

Ash, Mel. *The Zen of Recovery*. New York: Jeremy P. Tarcher/Putnam Book, 1993.

Webber, Meletios. *Steps of Transformation: An Orthodox Priest Explores the Twelve Steps*. Ben Lomond, CA: Conciliar Press, 2003.

Z., Phillip. *A Skeptics Guide to the 12 Steps*. Center City, MN: Hazelden Educational Materials, 1990.

ALTERNATIVE RECOVERY BOOKS

Berg, Insoo Kim and Scott D. Miller. *The Miracle Method: A Radically New Approach to Problem Drinking*. New York: Norton, 1995.

Christopher, James. *How to Stay Sober: Recovery without Religion*. Buffalo, NY: Prometheus Books, 1988.

Kasl, Charlotte Davis, Ph.D. *Many Roads, One Journey: Moving Beyond the Twelve Steps*. New York: HarperPerennial, 1992.

Kirkpatrick, Jean. *Turnabout: New Help for the Woman Alcoholic.* New York: Bantam, 1990.

Ringwald, Christopher D. *The Soul of Recovery: Uncovering the Spiritual Dimension in the Treatment of Addictions.* New York: Oxford University Press, 2002. (Note: This book discusses several recovery options, including the Twelve Steps.)

Trimpey, Jack. *The Final Fix for Alcohol and Drug Dependence: AVRT.* Lotus, CA: Rational Recovery, 1994.

SPIRITUAL GROWTH AND EXPLORATION

Huber, Cheri, *The Key: And the Name of the Key Is Willingness.* Mountain View, CA: A Center for the Practice of Zen Buddhist Meditation, 1984.

Booth, Leo. *The God Game: It's Your Move.* Walpole, NH: Stillpoint Publishing, 1994.

Chopra, Deepak. *How to Know God: The Soul's Journey into the Mystery of Mysteries.* New York: Harmony Books, 2000.

Kornfield, Jack. *A Path with Heart: A Guide through the Perils and Promises of Spiritual Life.* New York: Bantam Books, 1993.

McGregor, Jim. *The Tao of Recovery: A Quiet Path to Wholeness.* New York: Bantam Books, 1992.

Thompson, Peg, Ph.D. *Finding Your Own Spiritual Path.* Center City, MN: Hazelden Educational Materials, 1994.

WORLD RELIGIONS

Sharma, Arvind, ed. *Our Religions.* New York: HarperSanFrancisco, 1993.

Smith, Huston. *The World's Religions.* New York: HarperSanFrancisco, 1991.

Websites of Interest

The sites shown here appear to be genuinely objective. There are many others on almost any topic you can think of. Beware, however – even the most objective sites may have a particular slant or inclination in their writing, and some "spiritual" or "religious" websites disguise their intentions to lure new members to their organizations. (Perhaps that is why they are called "web" sites!)

WORLD RELIGIONS AND SPIRITUALITY

www.religioustolerance.org/var_rel.htm

www.mnsu.edu/emuseum/cultural/religion

www.clas.ufl.edu/users/gthursby/rel/

www.sightquest.com/health (use search word "spirituality")

www.belief.net (location of "Belief-O-Matic™")

ALTERNATIVE RECOVERY

www.ipass.net/a1idpirat/alternativerecovery.html

INDEX

44 Questions (online pamphlet), x
A Newcomer Asks (pamphlet), 16
acceptance, 84
agnostic, 77
    contingent in early AA, 24
agnosticism, 55, 57, 71
    advantages of, 77
    definition of, 77
Alcoholics Anonymous (book). See Big Book
alternative recovery programs, 146
amends, making, 120
anger, 71, 80–87
    accepting, 82
    effects of, 81
Anglican, 56
anonymity, 72
approval, seeking, 127
as we understood, 31, 41
    origination of, 25
atheism, 55, 57, 71, 75
atheist, 34, 75
    definition of, 72
attitude, 26, 32, 119
attitudes, 132
attraction rather than promotion, 21, 72
Baptist, 56
basics, back to, 142
Belief-O-Matic™, 59
beliefs, clarifying, 38, 43, 44, 47, 66
Beyond the Influence: Understanding and Defeating Alcoholism (book), 71
Bible, 78
Big Book, 39, 42, 79
blame, 122

boredom in later recovery, 130
brainwashing, 37, 96
Buddhism, 34, 57
Calvinist, 56
Catholicism, 56, 60
Cause. *See* God
charitable giving, 58
Christian Science, 57
Christianity, 56
Church of Christ, 57
Clancy I., 114
coincidence, 120
commitments, 142
compulsion, 115, 130
confession, 58
control, 116
cosmic garbage can, 117
creativity as an outlet, 140
daily reprieve, 135, 144
dancing, 58
dark night of the soul, 137
deity. *See* God
desire to stop, 32
despair in later recovery, 130
desperation, 144
dietary restrictions, 58
Divine Science, 57
Do You Think You're Different (pamphlet), 38
dreams, learning from, 46
Druidism, 57
Drunk's Prayer, 78
Earth-Loving Tree Hugger, 67
Eastern Orthodox, 56
Eastern religions, 57
ego, 34, 94, 118, 138

enlightenment, 58
Episcopal, 56
ethical behavior, 113
Evangelical, 57
evangelism, 58
faith, 52, 110, 112
fasting, 58
flagellation, 58
Four Absolutes (of Oxford Group), 24
Gnosticism, 57
God
    and group conscience, 95
    as we understood, 110
    aspects of, 30
    discarding old ideas, 79
    external personality, 102
    human characteristics, 42, 57, 76, 120
    in the Steps, 106
    in Twelve Steps, 18, 24, 69
    names for, 69, 76, 111
    personality. *See* human characteristics
    shame about, 78
    word as placeholder, 25, 107
Goddess Worship, 57
gratitude, 133
group
    and anger, 81
    as Higher Power, 33, 76
group conscience, 95, 100
groups
    who's in charge of, 93
Higher Power. *See* God
Hinduism, 57
hitting bottom, 143
homosexuality, 85
Houston Smith, 103
Huber, Cheri, 24
humility, 117
independence, 144
individuality, 93, 97, 99, 104

insanity, 109
interdependence, 144
Internet
    searching on, 58
    websites of interest, 58
intuition, 53
inventory, Fourth-Step, 114
irritability in later recovery, 130
Is AA a religious society?, x
Islam, 56
Jesus, 57, 78
Judaism, 56
leaders of groups, 94
letting go, 112
literature, Twelve-Step, 147
logic, 38, 51, 52, 124
Lutheran, 56
McGregor, Jim, 135
meditation, 46, 60, 123, 136, 139, 141, 142
    in Oxford Group, 24
    releasing anger, 82
meetings. *See* groups
memories, uncovering, 47
Messianic Judaism, 57
Methodist, 57
moral code, 49, 112
Mormon, 57
mystery, 27
naming your spiritual recipe, 67
Narcotics Anonymous, 78
Native American Spirituality, 34, 57
Nonviolent Atheist, 67
Norse Paganism, 57
Oxford Group, 24
Paganism, 34, 57
pain, spiritual, 138
Pantheism, 57
Pentecostal, 57
perfectionism, 116
Phillip Z, 117
pink cloud, 129, 130
poverty, self-imposed, 58

Power greater than ourselves. *See* God
power, source of, 32
powerlessness, 107, 110
practices, spiritual, 57
prayer, 58, 75
    childhood, 41
    Drunk's Prayer, 79
    uncomfortable with, 34
    writing your own, 143
Presbyterian, 56
proselytizing, 73
psychic changes, 117
psychochondriac, 121
Quaker, 57
rational thought, 45, 51
religion
    and spirituality, 27
    comparing your beliefs to, 56
    definition of, 28
    language of, 123
    organized, story about, 60
    overview of various types, 56
    without God, 30
Religious Science, 57
requirement for membership in recovery, 16, 32, 72
resentment, 122
resistance. *See* spiritual resistance
restlessness in later recovery, 130
retreat, 140
road rage, 126
sacred, 28, 50, 67, 103, 107, 124
sacred music, 143
sanity, 109
Scientology, 57
self-control, 108
self-criticism, 122
semantics, 111
serenity, 125
Serenity Prayer, 101
service, 94, 126, 132, 142
Seventh-Step Prayer, 118

sexual abstinence, 58
shame, 84
skepticism, 21
spirit, definition of, 27
spiritual
    adjustment, 139
    cleansing, 140
    combinations, 60
    condition, maintaining, 135
    definition of, 27
    enlightenment, 57
    experience, 102
    foothold, regaining, 130
    foundation, 23, 43
    obstacles, 39
    outings, 136
    practices, 57
    recipe ingredients, 60
    recipe, and the Steps, 67
    recipe, defining, 28, 43, 55
    recipe, naming, 66
    resistance, 29, 32, 70
    seeking, tools for, 59
    shifts, 141
    suffering, 137
spiritual awakening, 125, 127
spiritual loophole, 16, 17, 74
spirituality
    and religion, 27
    and sexual preferences, 85
    defining, 17, 51
    fading, 129
    influences from the past, 80
    refreshing your, 142
    unique, 71
    updating, 142
    without God, 30
sponsor
    and Step Five, 115
    deciding whether to keep, 87–89
    helping with pain, 140
    selecting, 87, 100
    trusting opinions of, 131

with different beliefs, 75
St. John of the Cross, 137
Step-Four inventory, 114
Steps of Transformation (book), 28, 43
Take What You Like and Leave the Rest, 87
television, 140
Ten Commandments, 49
The Key: and the Name of the Key is Willingness (book), 24
The Language of the Heart (pamphlet), 25
Tradition Eleven of Alcoholics Anonymous, 72
Twelve Step Programs, list of, 145
Twelve Steps, 105–27
    atheism and, 72
    influence of agnostics on, 74
    of Alcoholics Anonymous, 18
    translating with your idea of God, 69
    using another name for God, 69
    without God, 30, 73
    without spirituality, 30
Twelve Traditions, 21
Twelve-Step recovery
    agnosticism and, 77

agnostics in early days, 74
atheism in, 74
requirement for membership, 16, 32
spiritual loophole, 16, 17
without God, 36
Unitarian Universalism, 57
Unity, 57
values, 17, 38, 53, 76, 119
vulnerability, 144
We Agnostics (from Big Book), 39, 40, 41, 79
Webber, Father Meletios, 28, 43
websites, related, 150
whirling, 58
Wicca, 57
willingness, 32, 70, 72, 102, 144
willpower, 107, 116, 117
Wilson, Bill, 24, 31
Witchcraft, 57
World Wide Web. *See* Internet
www.belief.net, 58
www.positiveatheism.org, 72
Yoga, 57
Zen Judaist, 67
Zen meditation, 60